Our Next 250 Years

Incentives and Jobs

By

Charles Patton

About the Series

The **Our Next 250 Years** *series examines the forces shaping the future of American democracy. Across three volumes, Representation and Influence, Power and Control, and Incentives and Jobs, Charles Patton explores how political structure, institutional power, and economic systems interact to shape the nation's future.*

Our Next 250 Years – Incentives and Jobs

DISCLAIMER

This work examines the structural forces that shape governance, economic systems, and national outcomes. If I have misrepresented anyone's views, I welcome corrections.

I used referential terminology (e.g., forefathers, congressman, and he) when historically accurate while adopting more recent terms like congresspeople in later years as other genders gained recognition in these roles. I did not update punctuation to reflect modern standards or alter historical spellings in quotes or documents (e.g., chuse [sic]).

I relied on recent data for statistical references. While not always from the current year due to availability, the figures remain valid and reflect ongoing trends. Although political parties often differ on key issues, this book presents alternative perspectives without assigning them to any particular party.

This book is not about politics. It's about governance, how societies are best managed. When offering a position or recommendation, I have aimed for a fair and balanced interpretation of the facts rather than political persuasion, though I may argue for particular alternatives. In the spirit of our founding fathers, I advocate neither political party but only what I believe is best for America's citizens.

CREDITS

Written for and owned by: Applied Market Solutions, LLC

d.b.a. Short Mystery Press

Edited by: Dr. Geoff Patton

Cover by artist: Diogo Leite of D Design Company

Visit Charlespattonbooks.com to contact the author

ROLE OF ARTIFICIAL INTELLIGENCE (AI) IN THIS BOOK

As someone with dyslexia, I found OpenAI's ChatGPT and Google's Gemini (formerly Bard) helpful in refining, simplifying, organizing, and clarifying my writing, as well as in sourcing and fact-checking. However, I am solely responsible for selecting topics, structuring content, crafting prompts, forming opinions, formulating proposals, and writing.

Preface

This book is motivated by the condition of liberty as a fundamental right and by the obligation to preserve and protect it.

The country has changed. It has grown in size, complexity, and speed. Technology accelerates the spread of information and misinformation. Economic and political influence have become increasingly concentrated. The pressures on the system are not subtle, placing increasing strain on institutions and public trust.

These pressures are not temporary but long-term and, if left unaddressed, will shape the direction of the country for decades. Over time, they will determine whether the system remains stable, adaptive, and free, or becomes increasingly constrained and divided.

Renewal does not begin with institutions alone. It begins with citizens. Who are we? What do we stand for? Are we guided by convenience and self-interest, or by obligation to something larger than ourselves? A free society depends on citizens who understand that liberty requires participation, judgment, and restraint.

After leaving office, Jimmy Carter chose to be called "Citizen." The message was simple. A nation's strength rests not only in its leaders, but in the character and engagement of its people. Citizenship is not a title. It is an obligation.

The future of a free society is not determined at a single moment. It is shaped over time, through the decisions of its citizens and the structure of its institutions. The choices made today, and the incentives that guide those choices, will influence the direction of the system for generations.

This book is written for those who take that obligation seriously.

Introduction

America remains one of the most durable experiments in self-government. It has endured longer than most republics, not because it is perfect, but because it was built on structure, debate, and limits on power.

But the system is under strain. Many citizens no longer trust government, the courts, elections, the press, or each other. People sense that something is wrong, but they disagree about the cause and what should be done.

Much of the debate focuses on symptoms. Wages, jobs, inflation, inequality, and growth are treated as separate problems. Each is an outcome of the system. This book examines that system.

It focuses on how policy creates incentives, how incentives guide investment, and how investment shapes jobs, income, and economic stability. These relationships are not abstract. They shape daily life and the long-term direction of the country.

Policy sets the rules. Those rules create incentives for those who control capital and make decisions. Incentives guide where capital flows, whether toward production or financial assets, domestic investment, or offshore activity. Capital allocation shapes business decisions, including hiring, wages, investment, and cost control. Those decisions determine the availability, type, and stability of jobs. Jobs determine income, benefits, and economic security.

These conditions produce broader outcomes, including growth, inequality, and social stability. Those outcomes generate political pressure, which influences policy, and the cycle continues.

At its core, the system is simple. Incentives drive investment. Investment shapes jobs. Jobs determine income and stability. When incentives are misaligned, investment follows, and the effects appear in how work is organized and how economic security is distributed.

When these relationships are misunderstood, public debate stays focused on effects rather than causes. Policies are set without a clear understanding of how they change incentives, investment, and jobs, leading to unintended consequences that worsen conditions rather than improve them.

This is not a short-term issue. Incentives set the direction of the system over time. Small differences in policy, repeated over years and decades, shape where capital flows, how work is organized, and how economic security is distributed. Those patterns compound, influencing institutional stability and social cohesion.

The American system was designed with restraint. It assumes that power seeks more power. It assumes disagreement. It assumes competing interests. Its structure channels those forces within lawful limits. But that structure depends on citizens understanding how the system works in practice, not just in theory, and using the tools available to them—including voting, public pressure, and participation—to keep it within bounds.

The question is not whether the system will change. It will. The question is how it will change and whether those changes will preserve liberty, stability, and opportunity over time.

This volume is the third book in the *Our Next 250 Years* series. The earlier books examine the foundations of representation and the forces that shape policy, power, and control. Together, the series explores how institutional design influences economic opportunity, political stability, and long-term national prosperity.

The chapters that follow examine how policy, incentives, and investment interact to shape jobs and economic outcomes, how these relationships have changed over time, and how they influence the choices facing the country. To understand jobs, income, and inequality, the relationship between policy, incentives, capital allocation, and employment must be understood.

The following diagram presents that relationship in a single view.

Structural Drivers of Jobs, Income, and Inequality

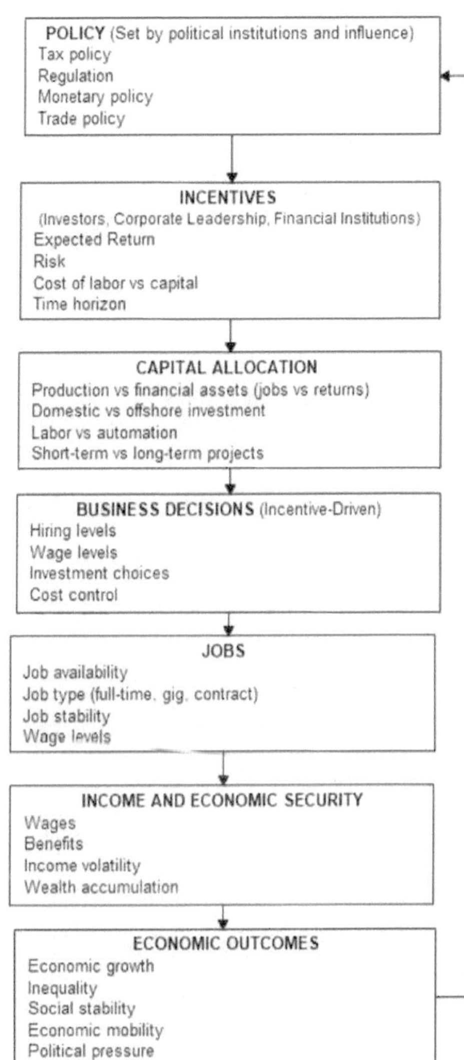

SECTION I — Policies and Incentives

Policies

Policy sets the rules under which decisions are made.

The Rules We Live By

Policy is not an abstract concept. It is the collection of laws, regulations, taxes, monetary actions, and trade rules that define how the system operates. These rules exist at multiple levels of government. At the federal level, Congress passes laws, agencies issue regulations, and the central bank sets monetary conditions. States and cities add their own layers through statutes, ordinances, and local rules. Together, these policies establish the environment in which economic and social activity takes place.

It's a Large Field

The scale of policy is significant. Federal spending in the United States exceeds $6 trillion per year, with state and local governments adding several trillion more.[01-06] The federal tax code spans more than 70,000 pages when regulations and guidance are included.[01-07] Federal agencies publish tens of thousands of pages of rules each year in the Federal Register, with the cumulative body of federal regulation running to hundreds of thousands of pages.[01-08] The Code of Federal Regulations alone contains more than 180,000 pages of rules.[01-09] The federal government operates through more than 400 agencies and sub-agencies that issue and enforce policy across the economy.[01-10] Monetary policy decisions by the Federal Reserve influence interest rates and credit conditions across an economy exceeding $25 trillion in annual output, affecting borrowing costs for households, businesses, and governments.[01-11, 01-12]

These policies do not operate at the margins but define the conditions under which most economic and social activity occurs.

Laws establish what is permitted and what is prohibited. Regulations define how those laws are implemented and enforced. Taxes determine how resources are collected and redistributed. Monetary policy influences the cost and availability of money. Trade policy shapes the flow of goods, services, and capital across borders. Each of these elements affects behavior, not by acting directly, but by setting the conditions under which decisions are made.

Policy to Incentives to Outcomes

Policy, in practical terms, is the set of rules that governs decisions. Most people think of policy in terms of intended outcomes. A law is passed to create jobs, reduce costs, increase growth, or address inequality, with the expectation that it will produce the stated result.

Complex systems rarely operate in that way. Policy creates incentives that shape decisions and produce outcomes.

Understanding this distinction is critical. Without it, policies are judged by their stated goals rather than by the incentives they create. Those incentives are often indirect, embedded in the structure of the policy, or not fully understood at the time. As a result, the actual effects of policy are often misunderstood, unanticipated, or obscured.

Policy works by changing the conditions under which decisions are made. It changes costs, risks, expected returns, and constraints. When those conditions change, behavior changes.

Behavior is expressed through actions. If the cost of an action rises, it becomes less attractive. If the expected return increases, it becomes more attractive. If risk is reduced, capital will move in that direction. If constraints are removed, activity expands. These are normal responses of individuals and institutions operating within a system.

For example, if a policy increases the cost of hiring by raising payroll taxes or regulatory requirements, businesses are less likely to add workers. If the same policy provides incentives for automation or financial investment, capital will move in that direction instead. Hiring slows, investment shifts, and the structure of jobs changes. The policy may have been intended to support workers, but incentives determined the outcome.

Motivation follows incentives. In economic systems, those incentives are often financial, but they also include power, influence, and control. Policy uses these incentives, intentionally or not, to shape behavior. The outcomes that follow reflect those incentives, not the stated intent of the policy.

Incentives also differ across decision-makers. Investors, corporate leadership, and financial institutions respond to expected return, risk, time horizon, and the relative cost of labor and capital. When the cost of labor rises relative to capital, investment may shift toward automation. When returns are immediate, short-term decisions are favored. When returns require time and carry uncertainty, long-term investment becomes less attractive. These factors shape how capital is allocated.

Not all actors respond to policy in the same way. The most significant responses come from those who control capital and make large-scale decisions, including investors, corporate leadership, and financial institutions. These actors determine where capital is allocated, which projects are funded, and which activities expand or contract. Their decisions have broad effects. When capital moves toward one sector, that sector grows. When capital leaves another, it contracts. Hiring, wages, and investment follow these movements. The structure of jobs and the distribution of income are shaped by these decisions.

For this reason, the incentives that matter most are those facing decision-makers who control capital. Their responses to policy drive the outcomes experienced by workers, households, and communities. Policies are often designed with specific goals in mind, aiming to increase employment, reduce costs, promote growth, or address specific problems. But outcomes are determined by the incentives created, not the intentions stated.

When incentives align with the stated goal, the policy may produce the desired result. When they do not, the results can differ significantly from what was intended. In some cases, they can produce the opposite effect. This is not an exception. It is a normal feature of complex systems. Policies operate through incentives, and incentives change decisions.

Policy sets incentives that guide capital allocation, business decisions, and the availability, type, and stability of jobs.

What This Means for the Next 250 Years

The structure of policy determines the structure of incentives. The structure of incentives influences how capital is allocated. Over time, these decisions shape the economy, the workforce, and the stability of society.

Small differences in incentives, applied consistently over time, produce large differences in outcomes. Policies that favor short-term returns will encourage short-term decision-making. Policies that increase uncertainty will reduce long-term investment. Policies that shift risk from institutions to individuals will change how work is structured and how income is distributed.

These effects compound over time, accumulating across years and decades and shaping the direction of the system. A clear example is the decision in the early 1960s to commit to the Apollo program. When President John F. Kennedy set the goal of landing a man on the moon, it was not just a scientific ambition. It was a policy decision that directed funding, research priorities, and national focus toward advanced engineering, computing, and aerospace development.

That decision created incentives. Capital and talent flowed into universities, laboratories, and private contractors working on space-related technologies. Companies invested in electronics, materials science, and computing. Skilled workers trained in these fields. Entire industries expanded to support the effort.

The immediate objective was achieved in 1969 with the moon landing. But the longer-term effects extended far beyond that goal. The technologies developed through the space program contributed to advances in computing, communications, materials, and engineering that continued for decades. The investment helped establish leadership in key industries and strengthened the country's technological base.

The outcome was not the result of a single policy decision producing a single result. It was the result of incentives that redirected capital and talent over time. Those shifts accumulated, shaping industries, capabilities, and economic strength long after the original objective had been met.

A different example can be seen in policies that shaped globalization and capital mobility beginning in the late twentieth century. Trade agreements, tax structures, and regulatory decisions reduced barriers to moving production and capital across borders. These policies were intended to increase efficiency, reduce costs, and expand economic growth.

They created incentives. Companies could lower costs by relocating production to lower-wage regions. Capital could move more freely to where returns were higher. Over time, investment shifted away from domestic manufacturing toward global supply chains and, in some cases, toward financial activities that offered faster or more predictable returns.

These changes did not transform the economy overnight but gradually unfolded. Factories closed, new facilities were built elsewhere, and supply chains extended across multiple countries. Workers and communities adjusted over time, often with delayed effects. Entire regions experienced long-term changes in employment, income, and economic stability.

The outcomes reflected the incentives embedded in policy. Lower costs and higher returns in the short term were achieved, but they were accompanied by changes in job design, income distribution, and the location of production. These effects accumulated over decades, reshaping industries and communities in ways that were not always anticipated when the policies were enacted.

In both cases, the results were not driven by intention alone but by incentives that directed behavior over time. The effects of those incentives compounded, shaping the path of the system in ways that became fully visible only after many years.

The next 250 years will not be determined by stated goals or intentions but by the incentives embedded in policy and how those incentives shape behavior over time. If those incentives support long-term investment, productive capacity, and broad participation, the system can remain stable and adaptive. If they encourage short-term extraction, concentration of capital, and increasing instability, the system will come under growing pressure.

Policy determines the path the system follows. Over time, that path defines the future.

Incentives and Market Design

Incentives determine behavior within the rules set by policy. Market design determines how those incentives are structured and how participants interact. Together, they shape how resources are allocated, how decisions are made, and how outcomes are produced.

Incentives Drive Action

An incentive is a condition that makes one action more attractive than another. It can increase expected return, reduce cost, limit risk, or remove constraints. Incentives guide behavior by making certain choices more likely. Individuals and institutions respond to these conditions as they pursue their objectives.

For example, if a government offers a tax credit for building a factory in a particular region, the expected return on that investment increases. Companies that might otherwise build elsewhere are more likely to invest in that location. The policy does not command the decision, but it changes the incentives that shape it.

In economic systems, incentives are often financial, but they also include power, access, influence, information, and control. A change in any of these can alter behavior. The form of the incentive matters less than its effect on decision-making.

Market Design Structure

Market design is the structure within which incentives operate. It includes the rules of exchange, the flow of information, the degree of competition, and the mechanisms used to set prices and allocate resources. Markets are not neutral. Markets are constructed and shaped by policy, regulation, and institutional design.

A market with open entry, transparent pricing, and many participants encourages competition and price efficiency. A market with restricted entry, limited information, or dominant participants produces different incentives, often favoring control, higher margins, and reduced competition.

For example, if licensing rules limit the number of firms that can enter a market, existing firms face less competition. Prices tend to remain higher and profit margins increase because fewer competitors are able to offer alternatives. If those barriers are removed and new firms can enter more easily, competition increases and prices tend to move closer to underlying costs.

Interaction of Incentives and Structure

The interaction between incentives and market design determines how participants behave. The same participants will behave differently under different conditions.

Incentives operate within the market's rules, information, and participants. A tax, subsidy, regulation, or policy change does not act on its own. Its effect depends on how it interacts with existing rules, institutions, and participants. The same policy can produce different outcomes in different markets because incentives, costs, and competition differ.

For example, a tax credit for new investment may lead to expanded production in a competitive market with open entry. In a concentrated market with limited competition, the same incentive may increase profits without expanding output.

Participants do not respond to a single incentive. Decisions about investment balance expected return, risk, time horizon, and the relative cost of labor and capital. When the cost of labor rises relative to capital, firms may substitute automation for hiring. When returns are immediate, short-term decisions are favored. When returns require time and carry uncertainty, long-term investment becomes less attractive. These factors shape how capital is allocated.

Time Horizon

Time horizon is a critical dimension of incentives. Decisions that produce immediate returns are often favored over those that require time and carry uncertainty. When incentives emphasize short-term performance, capital tends to move toward activities with faster payoffs. When incentives support longer horizons, capital is more likely to be directed toward projects that require sustained investment. The timing of expected returns shapes how capital is allocated.

For example, repairing a damaged bridge may generate little direct financial return beyond restoring its prior function. Building new infrastructure, by contrast, may involve years of planning, permitting, and construction before any benefits appear. If incentives favor immediate results, resources are more likely to be directed toward projects with quicker and more visible outcomes. When incentives support long-term investment, capital is more likely to flow toward infrastructure, research, and other projects whose benefits accumulate over time.

Price Signals

In a competitive market with clear information, prices reflect supply and demand. Participants respond to those signals by adjusting production, consumption, and investment. When information is limited or distorted, prices may not reflect underlying conditions. In those cases, incentives can lead to outcomes that diverge from expectations.

In some markets, a dominant firm acts as a price leader. When that firm changes prices, competitors follow. Prices can move independently of underlying conditions, reflecting coordinated behavior rather than independent responses to supply and demand.

Barriers to Entry

Barriers to entry shape incentives. When entry is easy, new participants increase competition and expand options. When entry is restricted, existing participants face less pressure. Incentives shift from competing on value to maintaining position. The result can be higher costs, reduced innovation, and limited opportunity. In the United States, industry concentration has increased across many sectors, with the largest firms accounting for a growing share of total sales and output. Research finds that more than 75 percent of industries have experienced rising concentration in recent decades, and that the share of sales controlled by the largest firms has generally increased over time.[01-13]

Market Concentration

Market concentration changes incentives. In a dispersed market, no single participant can influence outcomes. In a concentrated market, a small number of participants can affect pricing, access, and terms. Incentives shift toward control and coordination rather than competition. In recent years, a small number of large firms have captured a large share of corporate profits and market value, especially in technology and finance. For example, the top 10 percent of U.S. public companies account for roughly 80–90 percent of total corporate profits, while the five largest technology firms alone have at times represented over 20 percent of the S&P 500's total market value.[01-14]

Information

Information is a critical element of market design. When participants have access to clear and timely information, they can respond to conditions more effectively. When information is incomplete, delayed, or asymmetric, decisions are made with uncertainty. Incentives then favor those with better access to information, and outcomes reflect that imbalance. Financial markets illustrate this effect, where access to data, speed, and analysis can provide measurable advantages.

Risk Allocation

Market design determines how risk is distributed. Some structures shift risk toward individuals, while others distribute it across institutions or the public. These choices affect behavior. When risk is borne by those making decisions, incentives encourage caution and evaluation. When risk is shifted elsewhere, incentives can encourage expansion without full accountability. During periods of financial stress, government and central bank interventions have involved trillions of dollars in support to stabilize markets.[01-15]

Combined Effects

These elements are not independent. Price signals, competition, information, and risk interact. Changes in one area affect the others. Market outcomes reflect the combined effect of these conditions.

Incentives and market design together determine where capital flows. When projected returns are strong, risk is manageable, and barriers are minimal, capital flows in that direction. When returns are lower, risk is higher, or access is restricted, capital moves elsewhere. These movements determine which activities expand and which contract. Participants respond to the incentives they face within the markets in which they operate.

Market design shapes the incentives that guide behavior. Those incentives influence how capital is allocated. That allocation determines how businesses operate and how jobs are created, structured, and sustained.

Small differences in competition, information, and risk allocation redirect capital across industries, regions, and forms of investment. Over time, these shifts accumulate and reshape the economy.

When market design supports open competition, clear information, and long-term investment, capital tends to move toward productive activity that builds capacity. When markets are concentrated, information is uneven, or incentives favor short-term returns, capital shifts toward control, extraction, or financial activity with limited long-term impact.

These patterns develop gradually as incentives are applied repeatedly. Over time, they shape industries, the availability and quality of jobs, and the distribution of income and opportunity.

Incentives guide decisions. Market design determines how those incentives operate. Together, they set the direction of the system.

When incentives favor scale, control of information, and barriers to entry, market outcomes tend to concentrate profits and power in a small number of firms. This concentration is not temporary. It is the structural result of how capital is allocated and how markets are designed. If these structures remain unchanged, concentration will continue, shaping the distribution of power, work, and income. As control increases, competitive pressure weakens, capital becomes more selective, and opportunities narrow.

Over time, this creates a system that is more efficient at accumulation than at broad participation, increasing the risk of instability. Maintaining a productive and adaptive economy will require preserving competition, improving transparency, and aligning incentives with long-term investment rather than short-term control.

Business Decisions Under Incentives

Business decisions translate capital allocation into action. Firms determine how resources are used, how work is organized, and how output is produced. These decisions shape employment, wages, investment, and costs across the economy.

Business decisions follow incentives. Firms respond to projected returns, uncertainty, time frames, operating constraints, and costs. These incentives are shaped by policy and market design. When conditions change, behavior changes.

Hiring Levels

Hiring reflects expected demand, cost, and risk. Firms add workers when they expect sustained demand and when the expected return from expansion exceeds the cost. When demand is uncertain or costs are high, hiring is limited or delayed.

Labor is both a cost and a source of production. Firms balance capacity with cost. When labor costs rise relative to output, hiring becomes less attractive. When expected demand increases, hiring expands.

Risk affects hiring. Permanent hires represent long-term commitments. When conditions are uncertain, firms rely more on temporary labor, contractors, or flexible staffing. This reduces risk but lowers stability for workers. In the United States, contingent and alternative work arrangements account for roughly 10 to 15 percent of the workforce.[03-01]

Hiring reflects incentives, not intentions. Policies affect employment only through their impact on cost, risk, and expected return.

Wage Levels

Wages are influenced by productivity, labor supply, market conditions, and incentives. Firms set wages based on output value, labor cost, and available alternatives. When productivity rises, firms can pay higher wages. When labor supply is limited, wages increase to attract workers. When competition for labor is strong, wages rise to retain employees.

Firms also face constraints. Higher wages increase costs. If those costs cannot be offset by productivity or prices, firms limit wage growth, reduce hiring, or adjust other expenses.

Incentives shape wage structures. Performance pay, bonuses, and equity link compensation to results. These can align incentives, but they can also favor short-term performance. Differences are large. Executive compensation in large firms is often measured in multiples of average worker pay.[03-02] Wages reflect a balance between market conditions and incentives, tied to cost, productivity, and expected return.

Combined Effects

Hiring, wages, investment, and cost control are interconnected. A decision to automate affects hiring. A decision to raise wages affects costs. A change in demand affects all four.

These decisions result from incentives and respond to conditions created by policy and market design.

Business decisions do not determine outcomes at the system level but translate incentives into action. Through these actions, capital is deployed, work is organized, and production occurs.

Jobs, income, and stability follow from these decisions.

Capital Allocation

Capital allocation determines what is produced, where it is produced, and how it is produced. It links incentives and market design to real economic outcomes. Decisions about capital allocation shape the structure of production, the availability of jobs, and the distribution of income.

Capital Moves

Capital responds to expected return, risk exposure, time horizon, and structural limits. These factors are shaped by policy and market design. When conditions change, capital moves. Those movements determine which activities expand and which contract.

Capital allocation operates through choices. Firms and investors decide where to deploy resources. These decisions include whether to invest in production or financial assets, whether to invest domestically or offshore, whether to use labor or automation, and whether to pursue short-term or long-term projects. Each choice reflects the incentives within the system.

Production and Financial Assets

Capital can be directed toward productive activity or toward financial assets. Investment in production expands capacity, creates goods and services, and supports employment. Investment in financial assets seeks returns through price changes, interest, or financial flows.

In recent decades, the scale of financial markets has grown substantially. Global financial assets exceed $400 trillion, several times larger than global GDP, and U.S.

financial assets are multiple times annual economic output.[02-01] These markets offer liquidity and returns that compete directly with investment in production.

These choices are influenced by expected returns and risk. When financial assets offer higher or more predictable returns, capital moves in that direction. When productive investment offers competitive returns, capital moves toward production. The relative attractiveness of these options determines how resources are allocated.

The difference matters. Investment in production supports employment and long-term growth. Investment in financial assets can generate returns without expanding productive capacity or creating jobs at the same scale. When a larger share of capital is directed toward financial activity, the link between investment and employment weakens.

Domestic and Offshore Investment

Capital can be deployed within the domestic economy or outside it. Domestic investment supports local production, employment, and income. Offshore investment may offer lower costs, different regulatory conditions, or access to new markets.

Global capital flows are large. U.S. multinational firms hold trillions of dollars in assets abroad, and global foreign direct investment flows total trillions of dollars annually.[02-02] These movements reflect differences in cost, tax policy, regulation, and market access.

These decisions are driven by cost structures, tax policies, trade conditions, and regulatory environments. When costs are lower or returns are higher abroad, capital moves offshore. When domestic conditions are more favorable, investment remains within the domestic economy.

The movement of capital affects the location of economic activity. When capital flows offshore, production and associated jobs often follow. When capital is directed domestically, it supports local economic activity. These patterns influence employment, wages, and the distribution of opportunity.

Labor and Automation

Firms choose how to produce, relying more on labor or on capital in the form of machinery, technology, and automation. This choice depends on the relative cost and productivity of each.

Automation has expanded rapidly. Industrial robot installations have increased several-fold over the past two decades, and the global stock of robots now exceeds three million units.02-03 Advances in software, artificial intelligence, and machine learning continue to expand the range of tasks that can be automated.

When the cost of labor rises relative to capital, firms invest in automation. When labor is more cost-effective, firms expand hiring. Advances in technology also shift this balance by increasing the productivity of capital relative to labor.

These decisions change how work is organized. Automation can raise productivity and output, but it can also reduce demand for certain types of labor or change the skills required. The mix of labor and capital determines the types of jobs available and the skills needed to perform them.

Short-Term and Long-Term Investment

Capital can be allocated to projects with different time horizons. Some investments produce returns quickly, while others require time and carry greater uncertainty. The expected timing of returns affects decision-making.

Short-term incentives are significant. Public companies report earnings quarterly, and management performance is often evaluated on near-term results. In recent years, U.S. corporations have spent over $7 trillion on share repurchases, returning capital to shareholders rather than investing it in long-term projects.[02-04]

When incentives favor short-term performance, capital moves toward projects that produce immediate results. When incentives support long-term investment, capital is more likely to be directed toward projects that require time to develop, such as infrastructure, research, and capacity expansion.

For example, recent federal infrastructure legislation committed more than $1 trillion to transportation, energy, and public works over multiple years. This directed capital into long-term projects that require planning, construction, and maintenance. The result was increased demand for labor, materials, and services, supporting employment and economic activity over time, driven by capital allocation rather than policy alone.

The balance between short-term and long-term investment affects economic stability and growth. Short-term investment increases responsiveness and liquidity, but an emphasis on immediate returns can reduce investment in long-term capacity. Long-term investment supports sustained growth but requires stable conditions and tolerance for uncertainty.

Combined Effects

These dimensions of capital allocation are interconnected. Decisions about production, location, technology, and time horizon are not made independently but reflect the combined effect of incentives and market design.

When expected returns are high, risk is acceptable, and constraints are limited, capital moves toward those opportunities. When returns are lower, risk is higher, or conditions are uncertain, capital moves elsewhere. Those movements determine the structure of economic activity.

Capital allocation determines where resources are deployed. Those decisions shape business operations, the production of goods and services, and the organization of work. Jobs, income, and stability emerge from those choices.

Capital follows incentives. When returns are higher, faster, or more predictable in financial assets, capital moves there. When costs are lower abroad, capital moves there. When capital is more productive than labor, investment shifts to automation. Together, these decisions change the structure of the economy.

As capital accumulates, the balance shifts. Productive investments that create broad economic value are limited relative to the volume of available capital. When those limits are reached, capital moves toward financial assets, acquisitions, and short-term returns. Prices rise, ownership concentrates, and the link between investment and production weakens.

At the same time, capital accelerates the use of physical resources. When returns are high, extraction expands. The constraint is not capital but resources and capacity.

If these incentives remain unchanged, capital will continue to move toward the highest and fastest returns. Production competes with financial activity, labor with automation, and domestic investment with lower-cost alternatives. Over time, this concentrates income and control and weakens the connection between capital and employment.

The question is not whether capital grows, but where it is directed. If it remains focused on short-term returns and financial activity, the system becomes more efficient at accumulation and less effective at broad participation. Sustained growth will depend on aligning capital with production, resource capacity, and long-term value.

Jobs

Jobs are the result of business decisions, driven by how capital is allocated, how work is organized, and how production is structured. Employment is not created directly by policy. It emerges from the incentives that shape business behavior.

Job Availability

Job availability depends on demand, investment, and expected return. Firms create jobs when expanding production is expected to be profitable. When demand is strong and conditions are stable, hiring increases. When demand weakens or uncertainty rises, hiring slows or declines.

The scale of employment is large. In the United States, total nonfarm employment exceeds 150 million jobs, reflecting the cumulative effect of business decisions across the economy.[04-01] Changes in hiring at the firm level aggregate into broader changes in employment.

Job availability is uneven. Some sectors expand while others contract. Capital moves toward higher expected returns and away from lower-return activities. As a result, job growth is concentrated in certain industries, regions, and skill levels, while other areas decline.

Employment reflects the direction of capital. Where capital flows, jobs follow.

Job Types

Not all jobs are the same. Employment varies across full-time, part-time, contract, and gig work. These forms reflect different balances of cost, flexibility, and risk.

Firms choose job structures based on incentives. Full-time employment provides stability but carries higher fixed costs. Contract and gig arrangements offer flexibility and lower long-term commitments. When uncertainty is high or costs increase, firms shift toward more flexible arrangements.

These employment types show how firms manage cost and risk. Flexible labor allows adjustment to changing demand but shifts income variability and risk toward workers.

The type of job affects income, benefits, and security. Full-time roles often include benefits and stability. Contract and gig roles may offer flexibility but typically provide less security and fewer benefits.

Job type reflects incentives and market conditions.

Job Stability

Job stability is influenced by risk, cost structure, and time horizon. When firms expect sustained demand and stable conditions, they offer longer-term employment. When conditions are uncertain, they seek flexibility.

Flexible labor arrangements allow firms to adjust quickly. This reduces risk for the firm but increases uncertainty for workers. Layoffs, reduced hours, and temporary contracts are used to manage changing conditions.

Economic cycles affect stability. During expansions, job security tends to increase. During downturns, firms reduce costs through layoffs or hiring freezes. During the 2008 financial crisis, U.S. employment declined by more than 8 million jobs.[04-03]

Job tenure has declined in some sectors. Median job tenure in the United States is about four years, and shorter for younger workers, indicating more frequent job changes.[04-04] Workers are more likely to change employers, and firms are more likely to adjust staffing levels.

Labor market flows reflect this. Each month, millions of workers are hired, leave jobs, or are separated.[04-05] This provides flexibility for firms but reduces predictability for workers.

Job stability reflects a tradeoff. Greater flexibility for firms increases uncertainty for workers.

Wage Levels

Wages are determined by productivity, the supply and demand for skills, the organization of work, and the incentives and bargaining power within the system.

When demand for labor is high relative to supply, wages rise. When supply exceeds demand, wage growth is limited. Productivity matters. Workers who produce more value can be paid more while maintaining profitability.

Wages are also constrained by costs and competition. If wages rise faster than productivity or prices, firms adjust through reduced hiring, automation, or cost control.

Wage outcomes vary widely. Economic output has grown, but wage growth has not been uniform. Since the late 1970s, U.S. real GDP per capita has increased substantially, while median real wages have grown much more slowly.[04-07, 04-08] Differences in skill, industry, and the level of competition contribute to variation in income. The top 10 percent of earners receive about 45 percent of total income, while the bottom 50 percent receive roughly 13 percent.[04-09]

Job availability, job type, job stability, and wages are interconnected and respond to the same underlying incentives. Automation can reduce demand for some roles while increasing demand for others. Flexible labor affects both stability and wages. Changes in demand affect hiring and compensation. These outcomes result from the interaction of incentives, competition, and business decisions rather than policy or intent.

Jobs reveal how the economy functions, determining how income is earned, how households plan, and how economic security is experienced. The structure of employment reflects how incentives direct capital allocation and business decisions, which determine the availability, type, and stability of jobs.

The direction of employment follows incentives. When capital moves toward financial returns, automation, or lower-cost locations, jobs shift or relocate. When investment is directed toward production and capacity, employment expands.

Over time, this changes how work is organized. More roles become flexible, skill requirements change, and income becomes less evenly distributed. Stability declines where firms seek flexibility, and opportunities concentrate where returns are highest.

If current incentives remain unchanged, the connection between capital and employment will continue to weaken. Firms will produce more with fewer workers, rely more on flexible labor, and adjust more quickly to changing conditions. For workers, this means greater variation in income, stability, and opportunity.

Employment will follow capital. Jobs will become more flexible, less stable, and more unevenly distributed as firms reduce risk and shift it to workers. Stability depends on sustained employment. If incentives continue to concentrate opportunity where returns are highest, stability declines.

Investment Choices

Firms allocate capital across competing opportunities, expanding capacity, developing products, adopting technology, or acquiring other firms. Each decision reflects expected return, risk, and time horizon.

When returns are high and conditions are stable, firms invest. When returns are uncertain or risk is elevated, investment is delayed or redirected. The cost and availability of capital also matter.

Investment determines how firms evolve. Capital directed toward production expands output and employment. Capital directed toward financial activity increases returns without expanding capacity. Capital directed toward technology changes how work is performed.

The scale is large. U.S. nonfinancial corporations invest trillions of dollars annually while also returning substantial capital to shareholders through dividends and share repurchases.[03-03]

Time horizon matters. Long-term projects require stable conditions and tolerance for uncertainty. When incentives favor short-term results, firms prioritize quicker returns.

These choices determine which activities grow and which decline.

Cost Control

Cost control affects all operations. Firms manage expenses to maintain margins and remain competitive. Costs include labor, materials, capital, compliance, and overhead.

When costs rise, firms respond by seeking efficiencies, renegotiating contracts, reducing inputs, or changing production methods to maintain returns.

Cost pressure changes how work is organized. Firms reduce headcount, outsource functions, invest in automation, shift production to lower-cost locations, or adopt technologies that reduce labor requirements. Productivity can rise even as employment growth varies across sectors.[03-04] These decisions affect employment, wages, and the distribution of work.

Income and Economic Security

Income and economic security are shaped by how work is organized. Wages, benefits, and employment stability determine how individuals and households earn, plan, and accumulate resources over time. These outcomes reflect incentives, capital allocation, and business decisions.

Income is not determined by policy alone. It reflects labor markets, business decisions, and economic structure. Differences in income arise from variations in skills, demand, productivity, and access to opportunity. As these forces change, the distribution of income changes with them.

Wages

Wages are the primary source of income for most households, reflecting the value of work, the supply and demand for skills, and the conditions under which labor is employed.

When demand for certain skills increases, wages for those skills rise. When supply exceeds demand, wage growth is limited. Technology, capital allocation, and the level of competition shift demand across skills. Automation and artificial intelligence expand the range of tasks performed by capital, increasing demand for some skills while reducing demand for others. These shifts affect both the level and distribution of wages.

Wages are also tied to productivity. When workers produce more value, firms can pay higher wages while maintaining profitability. When productivity gains are uneven, wage growth is uneven.

Over time, output has increased, but wage growth has not been uniform. Differences across industries, regions, and skill levels contribute to variation in income.[05-01]

Benefits

Compensation includes more than wages. Health insurance, retirement plans, paid leave, and other benefits are a significant part of total income.

Employer-provided benefits account for roughly 30 percent of total compensation in the private sector.[05-02, 05-04] This share has increased over time, but the structure has changed. Earlier systems relied more on defined benefit pensions and employer-provided coverage. Over time, many employers shifted toward defined contribution plans and cost-sharing. Retirement and health risks moved from firms to individuals.[05-05, 05-06]

Benefits are tied to job structure. Full-time roles are more likely to include benefits, while part-time, contract, and gig roles often do not. Coverage varies by industry, wage level, and firm size.[05-07]

As employment becomes more flexible, access to benefits becomes less consistent. A larger share of workers must secure health coverage, retirement savings, and other protections independently. This shifts cost and risk to individuals.

Over time, this trend increases variability in economic security. Workers with stable employment retain access to benefits, while others face greater exposure to health, retirement, and income risk.

Income Volatility

Income stability is as important as income level. Even when average income is sufficient, variability affects financial security.

Income volatility arises from changes in hours, wages, employment status, and economic conditions. Workers in stable roles tend to have more predictable income. Workers in contingent or flexible arrangements experience greater fluctuation.

Economic cycles amplify this effect. During downturns, reduced hours, job loss, and wage pressure increase volatility. During expansions, stability improves.

Households adjust through savings, borrowing, or changes in consumption. When income is uncertain, planning becomes more difficult and financial stress increases.

As firms increase flexibility, income variability rises. Over time, a larger share of workers may experience fluctuating earnings, even when overall employment remains stable.

Wealth Accumulation

Income determines the ability to accumulate wealth. Savings, investment, and asset ownership depend on both the level and stability of income.

Wealth provides a buffer against uncertainty. It allows households to absorb shocks, invest in opportunities, and plan for the future. Without sufficient income or stability, accumulation is limited.

Differences in income lead to differences in wealth. Higher and more stable income supports savings and investment. Lower or more volatile income limits these opportunities and increases reliance on debt.

Wealth is unevenly distributed. In the United States, the top 10 percent of households hold roughly 65 to 70 percent of total wealth, while the bottom 50 percent hold about 2 to 3 percent.[05-03] Since the 1980s, concentration has increased as higher-income households accumulate assets more quickly.[05-03]

The composition of wealth has shifted toward financial assets such as stocks and retirement accounts. These assets are more concentrated among higher-income households and are more sensitive to market conditions. Wealth accumulation is therefore more closely tied to financial markets.[05-03]

Participation in asset ownership is uneven. Higher-income households are more likely to own assets that generate long-term returns. Lower-income households are more likely to hold cash or housing, limiting exposure to higher-return assets.

These differences compound over time. Households with access to appreciating assets benefit from growth and reinvestment. Households without that access accumulate wealth more slowly or not at all. Over time, this widens the gap.

Combined Effects

Wages, benefits, income stability, and wealth accumulation are interconnected. Higher wages can support savings, but instability can offset that effect. Benefits can provide security even when wages are moderate. Wealth can reduce the impact of income volatility.

This reflects the structure outlined earlier. Income and economic security follow incentives. When capital moves toward financial returns, automation, and flexible labor, income becomes more variable and less evenly distributed. When investment supports production and stable employment, income is more predictable and broadly shared.

Over time, this changes how households earn and accumulate. Wages depend more on skills that complement capital. Benefits become less consistent as work becomes more flexible. Income becomes less stable as firms shift risk. Wealth becomes more important as a source of security, but access to it remains uneven.

If current incentives remain unchanged, income will become more dependent on market conditions and asset ownership. A larger share of households will rely on variable income and individual savings to manage risk. Differences in access to stable income and appreciating assets will continue to widen.

Employment alone will not provide economic security. Stability will depend on whether income remains predictable and whether access to assets expands or remains concentrated. If current incentives persist, more households will rely on variable income and individual savings, increasing exposure to risk.

Economic Outcomes

Economic outcomes are shaped by how the system operates. Policy sets incentives, and those incentives shape growth, inequality, stability, and mobility.

Economic Growth

Economic growth reflects the expansion of output, productivity, and income. It depends on investment, innovation, and the efficient use of resources.

In the United States, gross domestic product exceeds $25 trillion, reflecting the scale of economic activity.[06-01] Long-term real growth has averaged roughly 2 to 3 percent annually, with periods of expansion and contraction.[06-02]

When capital is directed toward production, including infrastructure, technology, and capacity, growth tends to increase. When it is directed toward financial activity or less productive uses, growth may be slower or more uneven.

Growth is not uniform. It varies across industries, regions, and time. Broad-based growth can improve conditions across the economy, while concentrated growth can leave large portions of the population unchanged.

Over time, growth will depend not only on the amount of capital, but on where it is directed. Systems that support productive investment expand capacity. Systems that favor short-term returns may increase output without broad gains.

Inequality

Inequality reflects differences in income, wealth, and opportunity. These differences arise from the same forces that shape jobs and income, including capital allocation, technology, and competition.

As noted earlier, wealth in the United States is highly concentrated, with the top 10 percent of households holding roughly 65 to 70 percent of total wealth while the bottom 50 percent hold about 2 to 3 percent.[05-03]

When capital flows toward activities that reward specific skills or ownership of assets, income differences widen. Wealth accumulation compounds these differences over time. Access to education, assets, and opportunity affects who benefits from growth.

Inequality affects both current conditions and future outcomes. Differences in income and wealth influence access to education, investment, and opportunity across generations.

If current patterns persist, inequality will increasingly reflect access to capital and assets rather than labor alone.

Social Stability

Economic outcomes affect social stability. When employment is stable, income is predictable, and opportunities are available, conditions tend to be more stable. When outcomes are uneven or uncertain, tensions increase.

Labor market conditions can change quickly. During the 2008 financial crisis, U.S. employment declined by more than 8 million jobs.[06-04] Unemployment has ranged from below 4 percent in strong markets to above 10 percent during periods of stress.[06-05]

Job instability, income volatility, and limited opportunity affect expectations about the future. Differences across regions or groups can increase division and reduce confidence in institutions.

Stability reflects both economic conditions and expectations. As income becomes more variable and outcomes more uneven, maintaining stability becomes more difficult.

Economic Mobility

Economic mobility reflects the ability to improve economic position over time. It depends on access to education, opportunity, and resources, and is influenced by the structure of jobs, income, and wealth.

Measures of mobility show that outcomes vary widely. About 40 percent of children born into the bottom 20 percent remain there as adults, while fewer than 10 percent reach the top 20 percent.[06-07] Mobility has also declined. For children born in 1940, roughly 90 percent earned more than their parents, compared to about 50 percent for those born in the 1980s.[06-06]

Mobility differs by region, education, and family background. Access to stable income, education, and assets supports mobility, while limited access restricts it. When mobility is high, individuals can improve their position over time. When mobility is limited, outcomes become more persistent across generations.

If access to assets and stable income remains uneven, mobility will depend increasingly on starting position rather than opportunity.

Political Pressure

Economic outcomes influence political behavior. As conditions change, individuals and groups respond through political processes.

Growth, inequality, stability, and mobility shape expectations and priorities. When large groups experience limited opportunity or declining security, pressure for change increases.

Political pressure reflects the outcomes produced by the system. As conditions change, so do the demands placed on policy.

Economic outcomes feed back into the system. Outcomes influence political pressure. Political pressure affects policy. Policy changes incentives, and the cycle continues.

This feedback loop connects outcomes to decisions. It can reinforce existing patterns or lead to change. When outcomes align with expectations, the system may remain stable. When they do not, pressure for adjustment increases.

The system does not end with economic outcomes. It extends beyond them, shaping how resources are distributed, how institutions operate, and how decisions are made. It shapes public policy, regulation, and enforcement. It influences access to education, healthcare, and infrastructure. It determines how technology is developed and used, how resources are allocated, and how risk is managed. It affects financial systems, corporate behavior, ownership, and global trade. These issues arise from the same system.

The same incentives that guide capital and business decisions also shape economic, social, and political outcomes. When incentives change, outcomes change. When they remain the same, patterns persist and reinforce over time.

Looking ahead, these incentives extend across markets and institutions. If they continue to concentrate returns, risk, and ownership, those patterns deepen, increasing pressure on the system. If they align with broad participation and long-term capacity, the system can support growth, stability, and opportunity.

The System Over Time and Structural Variation

The system operates continuously, not as a one-time event.

System Direction Over Time

Over time, this cycle determines direction. The next 250 years will not be defined by a single policy, leader, or event but by how our system operates across generations. Small changes in incentives accumulate and produce large differences in outcomes.

Growth, inequality, stability, and mobility are not fixed but reflect repeated cycles within the system. When incentives direct capital toward productive investment, growth expands and opportunity increases. When incentives favor short-term returns or concentrate benefits, those patterns intensify.

The system adjusts in response to the outcomes it produces. When those outcomes align with expectations, the system persists. When they diverge, pressure builds. That pressure influences policy, reshapes incentives, and redirects its course.

Most change is gradual. Small adjustments shift incentives over time. At times, pressure builds faster than the system can adjust. Periods of imbalance or instability can produce more abrupt change, including major policy shifts or institutional reform.

Structural Channels of Change

The system can adjust within its structure or change how it operates. Structural changes alter how decisions are made, how capital is allocated, how work is organized, and how income is distributed. They change how the system functions and who bears risk.

Changes in governance alter how policy is set. More direct systems can increase responsiveness but also increase variability. Representative systems may provide stability but adjust more slowly. These differences change incentives and outcomes.

Changes in work structure alter the balance between flexibility and stability. Greater reliance on independent work increases adaptability but shifts risk to individuals. Systems that emphasize long-term employment provide stability but reduce flexibility.

Changes in income structure alter how risk is distributed. Systems that provide baseline income reduce volatility and increase security, but they also change responses to work and opportunity.

Changes in access to capital affect who can invest and build. Broader access expands participation. It also redistributes risk across the system.

These variations do not change the sequence. What changes is how each part operates and who benefits.

Change is not optional. The system will continue to produce outcomes, and those outcomes will create pressure. The question is whether change is deliberate or reactive.

The same structure carries into everything that follows. Trade, inflation, technology, labor markets, and other domains operate through the same sequence of policy, incentives, capital, and outcomes, differing in detail, not in structure.

Over long periods, small differences in incentives produce large differences in outcomes. The system will continue to evolve. As we move forward, if incentives concentrate returns, ownership, and control, capital will follow. Investment will shift toward financial assets, automation, and scale. Ownership will narrow.

Income will become more uneven. Risk will move from institutions to individuals. These patterns will extend into access to education, healthcare, infrastructure, and opportunity, increasing pressure across the system.

If incentives support broad participation and long-term capacity, capital will move toward production, skills, and infrastructure. Employment will be more stable, income more predictable, and access to assets more widely distributed, supporting sustained growth and stability over time.

Section II — Policy and Control Systems

Economic Policy and Strategic Tradeoffs

Economic policy is not a collection of programs. It is a set of choices about where risk sits, where gains accrue, and what the country can still do for itself when conditions change. Those choices determine not only growth but resilience under stress, defining whether the system can continue to function when inputs are disrupted, capital shifts, or external pressure is applied.

Scale

The scale of these decisions is large. U.S. gross domestic product exceeds $27 trillion annually, representing roughly one-quarter of global output.[07-01] Trade is a central component of that activity. Imports of goods and services account for approximately 14 to 15 percent of U.S. GDP, while total trade, imports plus exports, represents roughly 25 percent.[07-02] These flows are embedded in production, consumption, and supply chains across the economy.

Global integration has reduced costs and increased efficiency. It has also increased exposure. The United States imported more than $3.8 trillion in goods and services in 2024, including critical inputs used in manufacturing, energy, technology, and healthcare.[07-01] When those inputs are disrupted, the effects move through production, employment, and prices. Supply chain disruptions during the COVID-19 period reduced U.S. real GDP growth by an estimated 1 percentage point in 2021 alone, illustrating how external constraints can affect domestic output.[07-03]

Dependence

Dependence is not evenly distributed. Many sectors rely heavily on foreign inputs. In advanced manufacturing, more than one-third of intermediate goods used in production are imported.[07-04] In some critical categories, dependence is far higher. The United States is more than 50 percent import reliant for over half of the minerals designated as critical by the U.S. Geological Survey, and 100 percent import reliant for more than a dozen of those minerals, including rare earth elements.[07-05] These inputs are required for electronics, energy systems, defense applications, and advanced manufacturing.

Semiconductors illustrate the same pattern. The United States accounted for approximately 37 percent of global semiconductor manufacturing capacity in 1990. Today, that share is below 12 percent.[07-06] At the same time, a large share of advanced chip production is concentrated in a small number of locations, increasing vulnerability to disruption. These chips are inputs into nearly every sector of the economy, including transportation, communications, healthcare, and defense.

Energy

Energy provides another example. The United States has increased domestic energy production in recent years and is a net exporter of energy overall but still relies on global markets for pricing and certain inputs. Oil prices are set globally, not domestically, and disruptions in global supply affect domestic costs regardless of domestic production levels.[07-07] Economic exposure is therefore not limited to physical imports. It includes price transmission through global markets.

These patterns reflect a core tradeoff. Open markets increase efficiency, reduce costs, and expand access to goods and capital but also create exposure to external conditions. Domestic capacity reduces vulnerability but often at higher cost. Policy choices determine where that balance is set.

The issue is not whether to engage globally. The issue is which functions must remain secure under stress. Some sectors can tolerate disruption. Others cannot. Consumer goods can be delayed. Core systems cannot. Energy, semiconductors, critical minerals, defense capacity, and essential medical supplies affect whether the economy can continue to operate.

Strategic capacity is therefore selective. It does not require domestic production of everything. It requires control, redundancy, and the ability to operate when external supply is constrained. That may include domestic production, diversified supply chains, stockpiles, or strategic reserves.

Incentives and Risk

These decisions are shaped by incentives. Firms allocate capital based on cost, return, and risk. Global sourcing often reduces cost and increases return. Domestic capacity often carries higher cost and longer time horizons. Without policy alignment, capital will tend to move toward efficiency, not resilience.

This creates a gap between private incentives and public risk. A supply chain that is efficient in normal conditions may fail under stress. A system that minimizes cost may maximize exposure. The benefits of efficiency are realized continuously. The costs of disruption appear intermittently but can be large.

Recent policy reflects this shift. The CHIPS and Science Act provides more than $50 billion in incentives for domestic semiconductor manufacturing and research.[07-08] The Inflation Reduction Act directs hundreds of billions of dollars toward domestic energy production, manufacturing, and supply chains.[07-09] These policies do not replace markets but alter incentives to redirect capital toward domestic capacity and reduce exposure.

Tradeoffs

The same tradeoffs appear across sectors. In pharmaceuticals, a large share of active ingredients are produced outside the United States. In technology, supply chains span multiple countries and depend on specialized production. In manufacturing, cost differences drive location decisions. In each case, efficiency and resilience are balanced through policy, incentives, and capital allocation.

These decisions accumulate. Choices made over decades determine whether capacity exists when needed. Rebuilding capacity is slow and costly. It requires investment, skills, infrastructure, and time. Once supply chains and production networks are established elsewhere, reversing those patterns is difficult.

Over time, these tradeoffs extend beyond economics, affecting national security, political leverage, and strategic autonomy. A country that depends on external sources for critical inputs is exposed to disruption, whether from market conditions, geopolitical conflict, or deliberate action.

The system described in the prior chapters applies here. The same mechanism extends across the domains that follow. Trade, inflation, technology, labor markets, energy systems, and global competition all operate through it. Differences in outcome reflect differences in incentives and capacity, not different systems.

Over Time

Over long periods, these choices compound. Policy determines incentives. Incentives determine where capital is deployed, whether production is domestic or offshore, and whether capacity is built or allowed to decline. Those decisions determine whether the country can produce what it needs under normal conditions and under stress.

If incentives continue to favor lower cost and higher short-term return, capital will move toward global sourcing, concentrated supply chains, and specialized production. Domestic capacity in critical sectors will remain limited, and dependence on external sources will increase. Supply chains will be efficient in stable conditions but vulnerable to disruption. Shortages, price volatility, and external leverage will become recurring features rather than exceptions.

If incentives support domestic capacity, diversification, and redundancy, capital will move toward production, infrastructure, and strategic supply chains. Critical inputs, including semiconductors, energy systems, and minerals, will be more secure. Costs may be higher in the short term, but the system will be more stable under stress, with fewer disruptions and less exposure to external control.

These outcomes are not driven by individual decisions but follow from how incentives are set over time. Once capacity shifts, it is difficult to reverse. Skills, infrastructure, and supply networks take years or decades to build. Dependence can develop gradually and then become structural.

The next 250 years will be shaped by these patterns. Systems that prioritize efficiency alone will tend to concentrate production and increase exposure. Systems that align incentives with long-term capacity will maintain the ability to operate under changing conditions. The difference is not theoretical. It determines whether the system remains functional when conditions are no longer stable.

Tradeoffs are unavoidable. Policy and incentives determine whether capacity is built or dependence increases over time.

Taxes

Taxation is one of the clearest expressions of state authority. It determines how government is funded, but also how incentives are set, how capital is allocated, and how economic outcomes are distributed. Taxes do not operate only as revenue but shape behavior.

Scale

The scale is significant. Federal receipts totaled approximately $4.4 trillion in fiscal year 2024, or about 16 to 17 percent of GDP.[07-10] The composition of those revenues matters. Individual income taxes account for roughly half of federal revenue, payroll taxes about one-third, and corporate income taxes less than 10 percent.[07-11] These shares determine where the burden falls and how incentives are applied across labor, consumption, and capital.

Taxation therefore operates through the same mechanism described earlier. Policy sets tax structure. Tax structure creates incentives. Incentives influence capital allocation, labor decisions, and consumption. Those decisions shape income, investment, and economic outcomes.

Jefferson and Tax Structure

Thomas Jefferson approached taxation as a question of fairness and consistency. He argued that taxation should reach all members of society and be applied uniformly. He identified three bases for taxation, capital, income, and consumption, and warned against taxing the same economic activity multiple times through overlapping mechanisms.

The principle matters because taxation can be layered. Income may be taxed when earned, taxed again when invested, and taxed again when consumed or transferred. Whether this is considered double taxation depends on structure, but the effect is clear. The same economic activity can be taxed at multiple points.

Jefferson's concern was not technical. It was structural. If taxation is inconsistent or uneven, it alters incentives and shifts burden in ways that may not be intended. His broader concern was that concentration of wealth and influence could affect policy itself, allowing those with resources to shape the system in their favor.

That concern remains relevant. Tax policy affects not only revenue, but the distribution of economic and political influence.

Tax Incentives and Behavior

Taxes influence behavior by changing after-tax returns. Higher taxes on labor reduce the incentive to work at the margin. Higher taxes on capital reduce the incentive to invest. Taxes on consumption change purchasing behavior.

Capital is especially sensitive. Investment decisions depend on expected return after tax. Changes in corporate tax rates, depreciation rules, and treatment of capital gains affect where and how capital is deployed. When after-tax returns are higher in one activity or location, capital tends to move in that direction.

Labor responses are more complex, but measurable. Payroll taxes reduce take-home pay. Marginal income tax rates affect additional work and participation, particularly for secondary earners. Consumption taxes affect spending patterns, especially for lower-income households.

These responses do not occur in isolation but aggregate across millions of decisions, shaping production, employment, and income distribution.

Tax Structure and Distribution

Tax systems differ in how burden is distributed. Progressive systems increase rates with income. Flat systems apply a single rate. Consumption-based systems tax spending rather than income.

In the United States, the federal tax system is progressive at the top of the income distribution. The top 1 percent of households pay roughly 40 percent of federal income taxes, while the top 10 percent pay about 70 percent.[07-12] At the same time, payroll taxes apply broadly and proportionally, and consumption taxes at the state and local level are often regressive.

The combined effect is mixed. Different taxes apply to different bases, and the overall distribution depends on the full system.

These structures affect incentives. High marginal rates can reduce the return to additional income. Broad-based taxes can reduce consumption. Targeted credits and deductions can shift behavior toward preferred activities.

The question is not only how much is collected, but how the structure influences decisions.

Wealth, Capital, and Concentration

Consistent with these trends, wealth in the United States has become highly concentrated: the top 10 percent of households hold roughly 65 to 70 percent of total wealth, while the bottom 50 percent hold about 2 to 3 percent.[05-03]

Tax treatment affects these outcomes. Capital gains and dividends are often taxed at different rates than labor income. Deferral, step-up in basis, and other provisions affect how and when taxes are applied. These rules influence long-term accumulation.

The result is not determined by a single policy. It is the cumulative effect of incentives over time.

Redistribution and Stability

Taxation is also used to redistribute income and fund public services. Programs funded through taxes support education, healthcare, infrastructure, and income assistance. These affect both economic opportunity and stability.

Redistribution can reduce extreme disparities and support consumption by increasing the purchasing power of lower-income households. At the same time, it can affect incentives if it significantly reduces the return to work or investment.

The balance is structural. Systems that provide support without maintaining incentives can reduce participation. Systems that rely entirely on market outcomes can produce instability when outcomes become highly uneven.

Historical evidence shows that extreme inequality can increase social and political pressure. Tax policy is one of the mechanisms used to adjust that balance.

Excise Taxes and Targeted Policy

Taxes are also used to influence specific behaviors. Excise taxes on tobacco, alcohol, and fuel are designed to reduce consumption or offset social costs.

Sugar provides a current example. While not broadly taxed at the federal level, it is associated with higher rates of obesity and related health conditions. Estimates suggest that a one percent tax on sugar-sweetened beverages could raise hundreds of millions of dollars annually while reducing consumption.[07-14]

These taxes are designed to change behavior. The tradeoff is between public health objectives and individual cost.

Fiscal Balance and Debt

Tax policy also determines the relationship between revenue and spending. When expenditures exceed revenue, deficits increase. Persistent deficits accumulate into debt.

U.S. federal debt held by the public exceeds 100 percent of GDP, and total federal debt is higher.[07-15] Debt service costs increase as interest rates rise, reducing fiscal flexibility.

This creates another tradeoff. Lower taxes may support growth in the short term but increase deficits. Higher taxes increase revenue but may affect incentives. The balance affects long-term fiscal stability.

Agriculture and Structural Support

Tax policy alone does not determine outcomes in sectors such as agriculture. In 2024, median farm household income was approximately $99,000, with a majority derived from off-farm sources.[07-16] Many farms operate with thin or negative margins.

Structural factors, including market access, input costs, and scale, are as important as tax policy. Taxes can support or relieve pressure, but they do not replace underlying economic conditions.

Minimum Wage and Tax Interaction

Wage policy and tax policy interact. Minimum wage increases raise earnings for affected workers, particularly at the lower end of the income distribution. Evidence shows gains in hourly wages with modest increases, and limited short-term effects on total employment at the aggregate level.

At the same time, there are tradeoffs. Reduced hours, higher prices, and increased automation have been observed, particularly when increases are large relative to local conditions. These effects vary by region and industry.

Tax credits, such as the Earned Income Tax Credit, are often used alongside wage policy to support income without increasing employer costs. These combined approaches reflect different ways of distributing income through the tax system.

Basic Needs and Participation

A functioning system must support basic participation. Individuals without access to shelter, food, and healthcare are limited in their ability to work and contribute.

Programs that provide early support can reduce long-term costs. Evidence shows that housing stability, nutrition, and preventive care reduce expenditures on emergency services, incarceration, and chronic unemployment.

These programs are funded through taxation. The design determines whether support is temporary, conditional, or ongoing, and how it affects incentives.

Taxes and Long-Term Capacity

Taxation is not only about fairness or revenue. It shapes the structure of the economy over time.

If tax policy favors short-term returns, capital will move toward activities that maximize near-term gains, including financial transactions and cost reduction. If tax policy supports long-term investment, capital will move toward infrastructure, production, and capacity. These choices affect where production occurs, how income is generated, and how resilient the system becomes.

Over long periods, the effects accumulate. Tax incentives influence capital allocation. Capital allocation determines capacity. Capacity determines whether the system can operate under changing conditions.

If tax policy concentrates returns and reduces incentives for production, capital will concentrate and capacity will shift. If tax policy supports investment, participation, and stability, capacity will expand and resilience will increase.

Taxes are one of the primary mechanisms through which the system is shaped.

Monetary vs Fiscal Interaction

Monetary and fiscal policy operate through different mechanisms, but they act on the same system. Fiscal policy determines how resources are raised and spent. Monetary policy determines the cost and availability of money and credit. Together, they shape incentives, capital allocation, and economic outcomes.

Fiscal policy operates through taxes and spending. It directs resources to households, firms, and public investment. Monetary policy operates through interest rates, liquidity, and credit conditions. It influences borrowing, investment, and asset prices. Neither operates independently. Each affects the conditions under which the other functions.

Scale

The scale of both is significant. Federal outlays exceeded \$6.1 trillion in fiscal year 2024, while revenues were about \$4.4 trillion, resulting in a deficit of roughly \$1.7 trillion.[08-01] The Federal Reserve sets short-term interest rates and influences broader financial conditions affecting trillions of dollars in credit across the economy.[08-02] These policies operate continuously, not episodically, shaping behavior across all sectors.

Transmission Through the System

Both fiscal and monetary policy operate through the same mechanism. Policy sets incentives that influence capital allocation, production, employment, and income, with outcomes feeding back into policy.

Fiscal policy changes disposable income and demand. Tax reductions increase after-tax income, while government spending injects resources into specific sectors. These changes affect consumption, investment, and employment.

Monetary policy changes the cost of capital. Lower interest rates reduce borrowing costs, increasing investment and consumption. Higher rates increase the cost of credit, slowing borrowing and spending. These effects are transmitted through financial markets, banking systems, and asset prices.

The interaction matters because both policies affect the same decisions. A reduction in interest rates may encourage borrowing, but high taxes or regulatory uncertainty may offset that incentive. Increased government spending may stimulate demand, but higher interest rates may limit private investment. The combined effect determines outcomes.

Interest Rates and Capital Allocation

Interest rates are one of the most direct channels through which monetary policy affects capital allocation, determining the cost of borrowing and the required return on investment. When interest rates are low, borrowing becomes less expensive. This encourages investment in housing, business expansion, and financial assets. Asset prices tend to rise as discounted future earnings increase in value. Lower rates also reduce the cost of servicing existing debt.

When rates rise, borrowing becomes more expensive. Investment is reduced or delayed. Asset prices tend to adjust downward as discount rates increase. Higher rates shift capital toward lower-risk assets and reduce leverage.

These effects are measurable. The federal funds rate increased from near zero in 2021 to over 5 percent in 2023, raising borrowing costs across mortgages, corporate debt, and consumer credit.[08-03] Mortgage rates rose from approximately 3 percent to over 7 percent during that period, reducing housing affordability and slowing transaction volumes.[08-04]

Interest rates therefore determine not only the level of investment, but its composition. Low rates can support long-term investment but can also encourage speculative activity if returns on financial assets exceed returns on production.

Fiscal Policy and Demand

Fiscal policy directly affects demand through spending and taxation. Government expenditures on infrastructure, defense, healthcare, and transfers inject resources into the economy. Taxation reduces or redistributes disposable income.

The effect depends on timing, scale, and targeting. During economic downturns, increased spending or reduced taxes can support demand and stabilize employment. During periods of strong growth, expansionary fiscal policy can increase inflationary pressure.

The fiscal multiplier varies by type of spending. Infrastructure investment tends to have longer-term effects by increasing productive capacity. Transfer payments can have immediate effects on consumption, particularly for lower-income households with higher marginal propensity to consume.

Fiscal policy also affects expectations. Persistent deficits can influence interest rates, inflation expectations, and investor confidence. These effects shape long-term outcomes.

Debt and Sustainability

The interaction between fiscal and monetary policy becomes more significant as debt increases. U.S. federal debt held by the public exceeds 100 percent of GDP, and total federal debt is higher.[08-05]

Higher debt levels increase the importance of interest rates. As rates rise, the cost of servicing debt increases. Net interest payments have grown rapidly and are projected to become one of the largest components of federal spending.[08-01]

This creates a feedback loop. Fiscal deficits increase debt. Higher debt increases interest costs. Higher interest costs increase deficits. Monetary policy influences this loop by affecting interest rates.

At high levels of debt, policy flexibility is reduced. Fiscal policy becomes constrained by debt service. Monetary policy faces tradeoffs between controlling inflation and maintaining financial stability. The interaction between the two becomes more binding.

Inflation and Policy Interaction

Inflation reflects the balance between demand and supply, but it is influenced by both fiscal and monetary policy.

Expansionary fiscal policy increases demand. Expansionary monetary policy increases liquidity and reduces borrowing costs. When both operate in the same direction, demand can exceed supply, increasing inflationary pressure.

This interaction was evident in the period following the COVID-19 pandemic. Fiscal transfers and low interest rates supported demand, while supply constraints limited production. Inflation rose to levels not seen in decades, exceeding 8 percent year-over-year in 2022.[08-06]

Monetary policy responded by raising interest rates to reduce demand and stabilize prices. Fiscal policy adjusted more gradually. The timing and coordination of these responses affected the duration and intensity of inflation.

Inflation affects real income, savings, and investment. It reduces purchasing power and can distort decision-making. Controlling inflation requires alignment between fiscal and monetary policy, or at least avoidance of conflict.

Distributional Effects

Monetary and fiscal policies affect different groups in different ways. Fiscal policy directly redistributes income through taxes and transfers. Monetary policy operates more indirectly, but its effects are significant.

Low interest rates tend to increase asset prices, benefiting those who hold financial assets. Higher rates can reduce asset values but increase returns to savers. Inflation reduces real income for those with fixed wages or savings.

Fiscal transfers can offset some of these effects by supporting income for lower- and middle-income households. Tax policy can adjust distribution through rates, credits, and deductions.

The combined effect determines how gains and losses are distributed across the population. These distributional effects influence consumption, savings, and political response.

Coordination and Conflict

Monetary and fiscal policy can reinforce or offset each other. When aligned, they can stabilize the economy. When in conflict, they can reduce effectiveness.

Expansionary fiscal policy combined with restrictive monetary policy can lead to higher interest rates without sustained growth. Restrictive fiscal policy combined with expansionary monetary policy can limit demand while increasing liquidity, with uncertain effects. Coordination requires understanding how policies, markets, and institutions interact, not central control. Policies that operate in opposite directions can create volatility and reduce predictability.

Institutional Structure

In the United States, elected officials set fiscal policy, while monetary policy is conducted by the Federal Reserve, an independent central bank. This separation is designed to balance short-term political incentives with longer-term economic stability.

The Federal Reserve operates with a dual mandate to promote maximum employment and stable prices.[08-02] Fiscal policy operates through the political process, reflecting priorities, tradeoffs, and constraints.

This interaction creates both stability and tension. Independence can support long-term policy, but it can also lead to divergence between fiscal and monetary actions. The system depends on how these policies interact rather than on direct coordination.

Long-Term Effects

Over time, the interaction of monetary and fiscal policy shapes capital allocation, growth, and stability. Persistent low interest rates can encourage leverage and asset price growth. Persistent deficits can increase debt and reduce fiscal flexibility.

These effects accumulate. Capital responds to sustained incentives, not temporary conditions. If borrowing is consistently inexpensive, leverage increases. If deficits are persistent, debt grows. If inflation is not controlled, expectations adjust. The result is structural. The economy adapts to the policy environment, and reversing those patterns can be difficult.

System Implications

Monetary and fiscal policy are not separate levers but operate within the same system and affect the same outcomes. Their interaction determines the cost of capital, the level of demand, the distribution of income, and the stability of the system.

If fiscal policy expands demand while monetary policy accommodates it, growth may increase, but so may inflation and asset prices. If monetary policy tightens while fiscal policy expands, borrowing costs may rise, reducing private investment. These interactions determine where capital flows, how resources are allocated, and how risks are distributed.

Over long periods, the balance between fiscal and monetary policy shapes the trajectory of the system. Persistent misalignment can increase volatility and reduce stability. Alignment can support growth, manage inflation, and maintain flexibility. The interaction of fiscal and monetary policy determines where capital is deployed, how risk is distributed, and how stable the system remains. Over time, that balance affects whether growth is sustained or volatility increases.

Inflation and Monetary Policy

Inflation reflects changes in the price level, but it is not a single cause or a single outcome. It is the result of how demand, supply, and money interact. Monetary policy shapes the conditions under which inflation rises, persists, or declines.

Monetary policy operates through interest rates, credit conditions, and the supply of money. These tools influence borrowing, spending, and investment. Through those channels, monetary policy affects demand relative to available supply.

Inflation therefore follows the same structure described earlier. Policy changes incentives. Incentives influence borrowing and spending. Those decisions affect demand, production, and pricing. Outcomes feed back into policy.

Demand, Supply, and Price Formation

Prices rise when demand exceeds supply. This can occur because demand increases, supply is constrained, or both.

Demand increases when households and firms have access to income, credit, or liquidity. Fiscal transfers, wage growth, and lower interest rates can all increase demand. Supply constraints arise from limited production capacity, disruptions in inputs, or structural bottlenecks.

Inflation often reflects the interaction of both. When demand increases faster than supply can respond, prices rise. When supply expands, price pressure can ease.

During periods of sustained inflation, monetary policy has been forced to move hard. In the late 1970s and early 1980s, inflation exceeded 13 percent. The Federal Reserve responded by pushing the federal funds rate above 20 percent, with mortgage rates climbing into the high teens. Borrowing slowed, demand contracted, and the economy entered recession, but inflation was brought under control. The adjustment was not contained. Institutions built for lower-rate environments came under stress. Savings and loan firms, holding long-term fixed-rate mortgages funded by short-term deposits, were squeezed as rates rose. Losses followed, failures spread, and the federal government intervened. The lesson is direct. When inflation is allowed to build, restoring stability requires force. That force moves through credit, institutions, and employment, exposing weaknesses created under earlier conditions.

Not all inflation is the same. Demand-driven inflation reflects strong spending. Cost-driven inflation reflects higher input costs, such as energy, labor, or materials. Monetary policy affects both indirectly by influencing demand and expectations.

Monetary Transmission

Monetary policy influences inflation through several channels.

Interest rates affect the cost of borrowing. Lower rates encourage borrowing for consumption and investment. Higher rates discourage borrowing and reduce demand.

Credit conditions determine the availability of financing. When credit is easily available, spending can increase. When credit tightens, spending slows.

Asset prices affect wealth and spending. Rising asset prices can increase consumption through wealth effects. Declining asset prices can reduce spending.

Exchange rates influence import prices. A stronger currency reduces the cost of imports. A weaker currency increases import prices, contributing to inflation.

These channels operate with delays. Changes in policy may take months or years to fully affect inflation. This lag complicates policy decisions.

Money Supply and Liquidity

The supply of money affects inflation through its influence on spending. When the quantity of money grows faster than the production of goods and services, more money is available to purchase the same output, putting upward pressure on prices.

Measures of money supply expanded significantly during periods of economic support. U.S. M2 increased by more than 25 percent between early 2020 and 2022.[09-01] This increase reflected monetary expansion and fiscal transfers that increased liquidity in the system.

Inflation depends on the money supply and the velocity of money, how quickly it is spent. If additional money is held as savings, its immediate impact on prices is limited. If it is spent, the effect on demand is stronger.

Monetary policy influences both the quantity of money and the incentives to spend or hold it.

Inflation Expectations

Expectations play a central role in inflation dynamics. If households and firms expect prices to rise, they adjust behavior. Workers may demand higher wages. Firms may raise prices in anticipation of higher costs.

These actions can reinforce inflation. Expectations can become self-fulfilling if not anchored.

Central banks seek to influence expectations through credibility. When policy is perceived as committed to price stability, expectations tend to remain stable. When credibility is questioned, expectations can shift.

Maintaining stable expectations reduces the need for large policy adjustments. Loss of credibility can require more aggressive action to restore stability.

Policy Tradeoffs

Monetary policy involves tradeoffs. Actions taken to reduce inflation can affect employment, investment, and growth.

Higher interest rates reduce demand and can lower inflation but can also slow economic activity and increase unemployment. Lower interest rates support growth and employment but can increase inflation if demand exceeds supply.

These tradeoffs are not symmetrical. Reducing inflation often requires slowing demand. Supporting growth can be done through both monetary and fiscal measures.

The Federal Reserve operates under a dual mandate to promote maximum employment and stable prices.[09-02] Balancing these objectives requires judgment under uncertainty.

Recent Experience

The period following the COVID-19 pandemic illustrates these dynamics. Fiscal support increased household income and demand. Monetary policy maintained low interest rates and high liquidity. At the same time, supply chains were constrained.

The result was a rapid increase in inflation. U.S. consumer price inflation exceeded 8 percent year-over-year in 2022, the highest level in decades.[09-03]

Monetary policy responded by increasing interest rates. The federal funds rate rose from near zero in 2021 to above 5 percent in 2023.[09-04] This reduced demand, slowed inflation, and affected borrowing, investment, and asset prices.

The adjustment was not immediate. Inflation declined over time as demand moderated and supply conditions improved.

Asset Prices and Inflation

Monetary policy affects not only consumer prices, but asset prices. Low interest rates increase the present value of future earnings, raising the price of stocks, real estate, and other assets.

These increases do not appear directly in consumer price measures, but they affect wealth and investment decisions. Rising asset prices can increase inequality by benefiting those who hold assets.

Higher rates can reverse these effects. Asset prices may decline as borrowing costs increase and discount rates rise.

This creates another dimension of inflation. Monetary policy influences both consumer prices and asset prices, affecting distribution as well as growth.

Constraints on Monetary Policy

Monetary policy depends on fiscal conditions, global factors, and supply constraints for its effectiveness.

When inflation is driven by supply shocks, such as energy or supply chain disruptions, monetary policy can reduce demand but cannot directly increase supply. This limits its effectiveness and can increase the cost of adjustment.

Fiscal policy can reinforce or offset monetary policy. Expansionary fiscal policy can increase demand, making it more difficult to control inflation. Restrictive fiscal policy can support disinflation by reducing demand.

Global factors also matter. Exchange rates, commodity prices, and international supply chains affect domestic inflation. Monetary policy operates within these constraints.

Long-Term Effects

Over time, monetary policy shapes capital allocation and risk-taking. Persistent low rates can encourage borrowing, leverage, and investment in financial assets. Higher rates can shift capital toward lower-risk investments and reduce leverage.

These patterns accumulate. The structure of the economy adapts to prevailing interest rates and credit conditions. Reversing these patterns can be disruptive.

Inflation itself has long-term effects. Persistent inflation reduces purchasing power, distorts price signals, and can reduce investment in long-term projects. Stable inflation supports planning and investment.

System Implications

Inflation and monetary policy operate through the same system as other economic forces. Policy sets incentives that shape borrowing, spending, and investment, which in turn determine demand, production, and pricing.

The balance between inflation and stability depends on how these incentives are set and how they interact with fiscal policy and real economic conditions.

If monetary conditions support sustained increases in demand without corresponding increases in supply, inflation will rise. If policy tightens too aggressively, demand may fall below capacity, reducing growth and employment.

The objective is not to eliminate inflation entirely, but to maintain conditions under which prices remain stable enough to support planning, investment, and growth.

Over time, the role of monetary policy is to influence the balance between demand and supply, risk and stability. The outcomes depend on how policy is applied and how the system responds.

Corporate Influence in Politics

Economic power can translate into political influence. As corporations increase in scale, resources, and legal protection, their capacity to shape public policy increases. This relationship is structural. It reflects how incentives, access, and institutional continuity operate within the system.

The Scope of Influence

The Supreme Court's decision in Citizens United v. Federal Election Commission (2010) held that independent political expenditures are protected speech and cannot be limited in the same way as direct contributions to candidates.[547] Subsequent rulings reinforced this distinction.

Following these decisions, outside political spending increased substantially. Independent expenditures in federal elections rose from approximately $143 million in 2008 to more than $4 billion in 2020, an increase of more than twenty-five times.[548] Super PAC spending alone exceeded $2.1 billion in the 2020 cycle.

Lobbying represents a second channel of influence. Federal lobbying expenditures have exceeded $3 billion annually for over a decade and reached approximately $4.2 billion in 2023.[549] More than 12,000 registered lobbyists operate at the federal level, representing corporate, trade, labor, and advocacy interests.

Spending provides access, but influence is sustained through presence and expertise. Large organizations maintain continuous engagement with policymakers, while elected officials operate within election cycles. This creates an asymmetry in time horizon, information, and institutional memory.

Complex legislation often depends on technical input from industry participants. Those participants help shape the rules that govern their own activity. This is a structural feature of modern policy formation.

The Revolving Door

Movement between government and industry reinforces continuity of influence. Former legislators, regulators, and senior staff frequently transition into private-sector roles where their experience and relationships have value.

Between 2001 and 2021, more than 70 percent of former members of Congress who left office to work in the private sector registered as lobbyists or strategic advisors. This pattern links public decision-making with private incentives.

The effect is alignment. Private actors gain insight into policy formation, and public officials operate within a system where future opportunities are tied to relationships with regulated industries.

Regulatory Structure and Market Effects

Regulation can shape competition and barriers to entry. Complex, compliance-intensive rules increase operating costs. Larger firms can absorb these costs more easily than smaller competitors. This can raise barriers to entry and contribute to concentration. Across U.S. industries, the largest firms have increased their share of total revenue by approximately 10 to 15 percentage points since the 1990s, depending on the sector.

As concentration increases, so does the capacity to influence policy. Economic scale and regulatory design can reinforce each other.

The Scale of Resources

Large corporations operate at a scale that rivals or exceeds public institutions. In 2023, Walmart reported revenues of approximately $611 billion, larger than the GDP of many countries. Several U.S. firms generate annual revenues exceeding $300 billion.

These resources support sustained lobbying, legal action, public messaging, and political engagement across multiple levels of government.

Government authority, by contrast, is distributed across institutions, agencies, and election cycles. This fragmentation contrasts with the continuity of large private organizations.

Influence is therefore not only financial. It reflects sustained organizational capacity.

Sector Concentration

Political engagement is highest where policy affects large flows of capital. Finance, healthcare, energy, and technology consistently rank among the top lobbying sectors.

In 2023, the pharmaceutical and health products industry alone spent more than $380 million on federal lobbying, the highest of any sector. Energy and financial industries also rank among the largest spenders. The scale of potential impact drives engagement.

System Effects

Corporate influence operates within the broader system. When policy formation is influenced by concentrated economic power, the system can become self-reinforcing. Economic concentration can increase political influence, which can shape policy in ways that sustain that concentration.

This process can emerge without coordination. It follows from incentives, resources, and institutional structure.

Over time, concentration can affect responsiveness. When influence is broadly distributed, policy reflects a wider range of interests. When influence is concentrated, policy may increasingly reflect those with the greatest capacity to engage.

Influence will track power unless constrained. If economic scale converts into political leverage, control over policy will concentrate alongside capital.

Policy Domains and Influence

Corporate engagement affects tax policy, regulatory standards, environmental rules, labor law, trade agreements, and antitrust enforcement.

Participation alone is not corruption. However, sustained engagement can shape legislative agendas, influence regulatory design, and affect enforcement priorities.

In complex systems, influence often operates through persistence rather than direct control.

Labor and Counterbalance

Corporate influence intersects with labor representation. Private-sector union membership has declined from approximately 24 percent of workers in the early 1970s to roughly 6 percent today.[551]

This reduces the institutional presence of organized labor relative to corporate advocacy.

Policy approaches differ. Some emphasize strengthening labor protections and collective bargaining. Others prioritize labor flexibility and reduced regulation to support job creation.

These approaches reflect different views on how economic power should be distributed.

Media and Information Channels

Economic concentration affects information distribution. A small number of firms control substantial shares of broadcast media, publishing, and digital platforms.[552]

In digital advertising, two firms, Google and Meta, account for roughly 50 percent of U.S. market revenue. Platform control over algorithms and distribution shapes visibility and public discourse.

Concentration in information channels can influence how policy issues are presented and understood.

Transparency and Limits

Disclosure laws require reporting of campaign contributions and registered lobbying activity. However, certain forms of political spending can obscure original funding sources.

In the 2020 election cycle, more than $1 billion in political spending was routed through organizations that did not fully disclose donors.

Transparency proposals focus on disclosure, reporting standards, and ethical constraints. The goal is to preserve open participation while limiting disproportionate influence.

Toward Economic Structure and Power Distribution

Corporate influence exists within democratic governance and shifts the distribution of leverage. Economic scale provides sustained advocacy, policy expertise, and institutional continuity. These factors affect which policy options are developed, prioritized, or advanced.

As capital becomes more concentrated and more mobile, the range of feasible policy choices can shift. Understanding corporate influence is not an endpoint. It is part of understanding how economic structure shapes outcomes, including jobs, income, and stability.

Banking and Financial Control

As economic value becomes more concentrated, control over credit, capital flows, and liquidity becomes a primary mechanism through which power is exercised. These functions determine who can borrow, invest, expand, or survive, shaping which activities grow or contract and how risk is distributed across the system.

Centralized Banking – The Fed

Debate over centralized banking authority dates to the founding of the republic. The Second Bank of the United States, chartered in 1816, served as a repository for federal funds, acted as the government's fiscal agent, and helped regulate state banks and currency stability.[59-30]

When Andrew Jackson became president, he moved to rescind the bank's federal charter. In his veto message, he argued that the bank concentrated the nation's financial strength in a single institution, exposed the government to potential foreign influence, benefited wealthy commercial interests over farmers and laborers, exercised undue influence over Congress, and favored certain regions over others. Like Thomas Jefferson, Jackson supported an agricultural republic and believed centralized finance favored an elite circle of commercial and industrial interests. After a prolonged political struggle, he vetoed the bank's recharter in 1832 and withdrew federal funds in 1833.[181-03]

The period that followed illustrated the difficulty of balancing stability and decentralization. Federal funds were placed in state banks, credit expanded rapidly, and much of it was weakly backed. Speculation increased, and when monetary conditions tightened, the system came under strain. Bank failures followed, contributing to the Panic of 1837.[181-03] Subsequent efforts to manage federal funds, including the Independent Treasury Act of 1846, shifted control but did not eliminate cycles of expansion and contraction.[181-05]

These recurring episodes led to the creation of the Federal Reserve System in 1913. The Federal Reserve was designed to regulate the money supply, reduce banking panics, and manage economic conditions through interest rates, reserve requirements, and liquidity provision. Its decisions affect the cost and availability of credit across the entire economy. Changes in rates influence borrowing, investment, employment, and asset values simultaneously. Although Congress retains oversight authority, day-to-day decisions are not subject to direct approval by elected officials, placing significant economic influence within a relatively small group of policymakers.

Debate over the proper role of central banking continues. Supporters argue that intervention during periods of stress, including liquidity support and emergency lending, can prevent broader economic collapse and preserve employment. Critics argue that such actions can distort market discipline, protect poorly managed institutions, and encourage excessive risk-taking. When losses are expected to be absorbed beyond the firm, incentives can shift toward greater risk. This dynamic, often described as moral hazard, reflects the tension between stability and accountability.

SEC

Control over financial markets extends beyond central banking to regulatory institutions. While the Federal Reserve influences the supply and cost of capital, regulatory agencies influence how that capital is used. The Securities and Exchange Commission was established to protect investors and maintain fair and orderly markets. It enforces rules governing disclosure, fraud, insider trading, and market manipulation in order to sustain confidence in financial markets.

Despite its authority, the SEC has faced criticism over missed warning signs and oversight failures, including the Bernard Madoff case. In response, enforcement tools have been expanded, including a strengthened whistleblower program designed to encourage reporting of misconduct. As markets evolve, the scope of regulation has expanded as well. Proposed and enacted disclosure requirements addressing environmental, governance, and social risks reflect an effort to capture longer-term financial exposures, though critics argue that such mandates may extend beyond traditional financial oversight. The challenge is to protect investors and maintain trust without imposing burdens that restrict participation or innovation.

Financial markets themselves concentrate control through capital allocation. Wall Street functions as a central marketplace for raising capital, pricing risk, and distributing investment across the economy. It provides liquidity and enables expansion, but it also concentrates influence. Decisions about where capital flows determine which firms grow, which contract, and how risk is distributed. Managing client assets creates inherent conflicts of interest. Oversight mechanisms attempt to limit these conflicts, yet periods of excessive speculation and misaligned incentives continue to produce cycles of expansion and correction. The scale of major financial institutions amplifies this effect. Large firms play essential roles in credit markets and global finance, but their size also increases systemic risk.

The financial crisis of 2007 to 2008 exposed these vulnerabilities. In response, the Dodd-Frank Act imposed stricter oversight on large institutions and introduced measures such as the Volcker Rule to limit speculative trading with depositor funds. These reforms sought to reduce systemic risk, but debate continues over their effectiveness. Some argue that stronger regulation is necessary to prevent instability, while others contend that excessive restrictions can reduce credit availability and limit economic growth.

Modern financial markets also rely on increasingly complex and rapid trading systems. High-frequency trading uses algorithms to execute transactions at extremely high speeds, increasing liquidity and market efficiency, but also concentrating advantage among firms with technological capacity. Speed and information asymmetry can create imbalances in market access and influence. Derivatives markets, including futures and options, provide tools for managing risk, but their complexity and opacity can amplify systemic exposure.

Limited transparency in these markets contributed to instability during the financial crisis, leading to reforms such as centralized clearing and enhanced reporting requirements. Credit rating agencies, whose assessments influence capital allocation, have also faced scrutiny for conflicts of interest, particularly when compensation structures align ratings with issuance rather than long-term risk.

Structural reforms have been proposed to address these issues, including separating retail banking from investment banking, as was done under the Glass-Steagall Act of 1933 before its repeal in 1999. Supporters of renewed separation argue that it could reduce conflicts of interest and limit exposure of depositor funds to speculative activity. Critics argue that such separation could reduce efficiency and competitiveness in global markets. Each approach reflects a different balance between stability, efficiency, and concentration of risk.

Control over capital is increasingly tied to the form of money itself. The integrity of U.S. currency remains a national interest, requiring continuous adaptation to counterfeiting and financial crime. At the same time, the system is shifting toward electronic transactions. Credit cards, digital payment platforms, and cryptocurrencies provide speed and convenience, but they also introduce new vulnerabilities. Cybersecurity risks, fraud, and system failures can disrupt access to funds. Digital systems can also increase the ability to monitor, restrict, or condition transactions. Control over payment systems can extend beyond processing to influence who can participate in economic activity and under what conditions.

Financial Control

These developments extend the reach of financial control. Credit availability, payment systems, regulatory structures, and market access all influence how individuals and firms participate in the economy. When access to capital and liquidity is stable and broadly available, investment and growth can expand across sectors. When access is constrained or uneven, opportunity becomes concentrated, and adjustment occurs through contraction rather than expansion.

Control over credit and capital extends beyond financial institutions. It shapes how businesses expand, how governments respond to crises, and how individuals access opportunity. Interest rates, liquidity, and regulation determine which risks are supported and which are constrained. When that control is concentrated, decisions affecting the entire economy can be influenced by a relatively small number of institutions and policymakers. When it is more widely distributed, adjustment occurs across a broader set of participants.

Over time, these structures determine how the system responds under stress. Systems that concentrate financial control can respond quickly, but they also amplify the consequences of error. Systems that distribute access and risk more broadly may adjust more gradually, but they can absorb shocks more effectively. The balance between efficiency and resilience is not fixed. It is determined by how control over capital is structured across the system.

Regulation and Administrative Authority

Regulation defines how laws are applied in practice. While legislatures establish statutory frameworks, administrative agencies develop, interpret, and enforce the rules that govern day-to-day economic activity. This authority extends across financial markets, labor standards, environmental protections, healthcare, energy, and communications. As economic activity has expanded in scale and complexity, administrative authority has grown in parallel, shaping how policy operates in practice.

Administrative Agencies

Administrative agencies exercise delegated authority. Congress establishes broad objectives and grants agencies the power to issue rules, conduct oversight, and enforce compliance. This delegation allows specialized institutions to address technical issues that may be impractical to manage through legislation alone. Agencies develop regulations through formal rulemaking processes, including notice and public comment, and they adjudicate disputes and impose penalties. These functions combine legislative, executive, and quasi-judicial roles within a single institutional framework.

The scale of regulation is substantial. The Code of Federal Regulations now exceeds 185,000 pages, reflecting decades of accumulated rulemaking across agencies.[09-05] Federal agencies issue thousands of final rules each year, affecting industries ranging from finance and healthcare to transportation and energy.[09-06] The estimated annual cost of federal regulation is frequently measured in the hundreds of billions of dollars, with some analyses placing total compliance costs above $1 trillion annually.[09-07] These costs influence pricing, investment decisions, and the level of competition.

Regulation affects firms unevenly. Larger firms are more likely to maintain legal, compliance, and regulatory affairs teams capable of navigating complex requirements. Smaller firms often face higher relative compliance costs. Surveys of small businesses consistently identify regulatory burden as a significant constraint on growth and hiring.[09-08] These differences can create barriers to entry, limit competition, and reinforce the position of established firms. Over time, regulatory structure can contribute to market concentration, not by design, but as a consequence of how costs are distributed.

Administrative Authority

Administrative authority also affects how quickly policy can adapt. Agencies can respond to changing conditions through rulemaking, guidance, and enforcement priorities without requiring new legislation. During the 2008 financial crisis and the COVID-19 pandemic, federal agencies implemented emergency measures affecting credit markets, lending programs, and industry operations within weeks.[09-09] This flexibility can stabilize markets and respond to emerging risks, but it also concentrates decision-making authority in unelected institutions.

The interaction between regulation and economic incentives is central. Regulations can protect consumers, workers, and markets by setting standards for safety, transparency, and competition but can also alter incentives by changing cost structures, limiting certain activities, or requiring specific practices. For example, capital requirements for banks affect lending capacity, environmental regulations influence energy investment, and healthcare rules shape insurance markets. These rules do not directly produce outcomes, but they determine the conditions under which decisions are made.

Influence in the Process

The process of regulation is influenced by participation. Federal lobbying expenditures have exceeded $3 billion annually for more than a decade and surpassed $4 billion in 2023.[549] Thousands of organizations submit comments during rulemaking processes and engage with agencies on an ongoing basis. Entities with greater resources and technical expertise are better positioned to participate consistently. Over time, this affects how rules are written, interpreted, and applied. Influence in regulatory processes reflects capacity for sustained engagement rather than formal authority alone.

Administrative authority also includes enforcement discretion. Agencies determine priorities, allocate resources, and interpret statutory mandates in ways that can affect entire sectors. Enforcement actions can signal acceptable practices and alter risk calculations beyond the specific cases addressed. For example, financial penalties, consent decrees, and regulatory settlements can reach billions of dollars, influencing industry behavior across markets.[09-10] Changes in leadership or policy direction can shift enforcement priorities, leading to variation in how rules are applied over time.

The growth of administrative authority reflects the increasing complexity of modern economic systems. Financial markets, global supply chains, digital platforms, and environmental systems require specialized oversight. At the same time, the concentration of rulemaking and enforcement authority raises structural questions about accountability. Agency officials are not directly elected, yet their decisions can have broad economic impact. Oversight mechanisms include congressional review, judicial challenge, and executive direction, but the balance between expertise and accountability remains contested.

Judicial interpretation plays a role in defining the scope of administrative authority. Courts have historically granted agencies deference in interpreting statutes within their jurisdiction, though recent decisions have limited that deference and emphasized the role of Congress in defining major policy questions.[09-11] Courts have historically granted agencies deference in interpreting statutes within their jurisdiction, particularly under the framework established in Chevron U.S.A. v. Natural Resources Defense Council (1984).[09-12] Recent decisions have limited that deference and emphasized the role of Congress in defining major policy questions.[09-13]

These shifts can affect how broadly agencies may interpret their authority and how regulations are developed and enforced.

Regulation and administrative authority operate within the broader system described in earlier chapters. Policy establishes objectives, but regulation determines how those objectives translate into incentives. Those incentives direct capital allocation, business decisions, and economic outcomes. The design, complexity, and enforcement of regulation therefore affect how the system functions in practice, not just in theory.

Over time, administrative structures influence how the system evolves. When regulatory frameworks are stable and predictable, firms can plan, invest, and expand. When rules are complex, inconsistent, or subject to rapid change, uncertainty increases, and decision-making shifts toward shorter time horizons. Regulatory structure shapes the range of choices available and the conditions under which those choices are made.

Public Spending and Fiscal Allocation

Public spending determines where resources are directed across the economy.

Size and Composition of Spending

While taxation defines how funds are collected, spending determines how they are deployed, affecting demand, investment, employment, and long-term capacity, and determining which risks are absorbed collectively and which are borne by individuals and firms.

Federal spending in the United States exceeds $6 trillion annually, representing roughly 23 to 25 percent of gross domestic product. Mandatory spending, including entitlement programs, accounts for the majority of federal outlays, while discretionary spending is determined through the annual appropriations process.

Short-Term vs Long-Term Allocation

Spending decisions allocate resources across time as well as across sectors. Programs such as Social Security and Medicare provide income and healthcare to current beneficiaries, while investments in infrastructure, education, and research affect future productivity. The balance between consumption and investment shapes long-term economic capacity. When a larger share of spending is directed toward immediate transfers, current demand may increase, but long-term growth depends on the level of investment in productive assets.

Effects on Demand

Fiscal allocation affects economic activity through demand. Government spending directly increases demand for goods and services, supporting employment and income. During periods of economic contraction, increased public spending can offset declines in private demand. During expansions, sustained spending can contribute to inflationary pressure if it exceeds the economy's productive capacity.

Investment vs Transfer Spending

The composition of spending matters as much as the level. Investment in infrastructure, research, and human capital can increase productivity and support long-term growth. For example, federal infrastructure legislation enacted in 2021 authorized approximately $1.2 trillion in spending on transportation, energy, water systems, and broadband over multiple years.[10-03] These investments can increase efficiency, reduce costs, and expand economic capacity over time.

In contrast, transfer payments redistribute income without directly increasing productive capacity. Programs such as Social Security, unemployment insurance, and income support provide stability and reduce poverty, particularly during economic downturns. These programs can also stabilize demand by maintaining household spending, but they do not directly expand production.

Distribution of Risk

Public spending also allocates risk. Programs such as unemployment insurance, disaster relief, healthcare support, and financial system stabilization shift risk from individuals and firms to the broader public. During the 2008 financial crisis and the COVID-19 pandemic, federal programs provided trillions of dollars in support to households, businesses, and financial institutions.[10-04] These actions were intended to prevent broader economic collapse, but they also increased federal debt and raised questions about long-term fiscal capacity.

Debt and Interest Obligations

The scale of federal debt reflects cumulative fiscal decisions. As of 2024, federal debt held by the public exceeds 100 percent of GDP.[10-05] Interest payments on this debt have increased as interest rates have risen, exceeding $800 billion annually and becoming one of the largest categories of federal spending.[10-06] As debt increases, a larger share of future resources is allocated to interest payments rather than current programs or investment.

Government Borrowing and Capital Markets

Persistent deficits require financing through borrowing. When government borrowing increases, it can affect interest rates, capital allocation, and investment. In some conditions, government borrowing can crowd out private investment by increasing the cost of capital. In other conditions, particularly when private demand is weak, government borrowing can support economic activity without significantly affecting private investment.

Interaction with Monetary Policy

Fiscal policy interacts with monetary policy. Government spending increases demand, while central banks influence interest rates and liquidity. When fiscal expansion is combined with accommodative monetary policy, the effects on demand can be amplified. When monetary policy tightens, higher interest rates increase the cost of borrowing for both the government and the private sector.

Distributional Outcomes

Spending decisions also influence distribution. Public expenditures on healthcare, education, housing, and income support affect the distribution of resources across households and regions. Differences in spending priorities can affect access to services, economic opportunity, and long-term outcomes.

Political Determination of Spending

The allocation of spending reflects political priorities. Budget decisions are shaped by legislative processes, negotiation, and competing interests. Programs with established constituencies tend to be more stable, while discretionary programs may change with shifting priorities.

Long-Term Fiscal Pressures

Long-term fiscal sustainability depends on the relationship between spending, revenue, and economic growth. When spending consistently exceeds revenue, debt accumulates. If economic growth outpaces the growth of debt, the burden can remain manageable. If debt grows faster than the economy, fiscal constraints may increase, limiting future policy options. Demographic changes, including an aging population, place additional pressure on programs such as Social Security and Medicare, increasing projected spending relative to revenue.[10-07]

System Effects of Spending

Public spending is part of a broader system that includes taxation, regulation, monetary policy, and competition. Spending decisions influence incentives, shaping capital allocation and economic behavior.

Over time, fiscal allocation shapes the structure of the economy. It determines which sectors expand, which risks are socialized, and how resources are distributed across generations. Decisions about spending do not only affect current outcomes but also influence the system's capacity to adapt, invest, and respond to future conditions.

The structure of public spending reflects how resources are allocated, how risk is managed, and how the balance between current needs and future capacity is set.

Debt and Fiscal Sustainability

Public debt reflects the cumulative difference between government spending and revenue.

Level and Growth of Debt

When spending exceeds revenue, deficits occur. Over time, those deficits accumulate into debt. As of 2024, U.S. federal debt held by the public exceeds $26 trillion, representing more than 100 percent of gross domestic product.[11-01] Total gross federal debt exceeds $34 trillion.[11-02]

Debt levels have increased significantly over the past two decades. Federal debt held by the public was approximately 35 percent of GDP in 2007, rose to about 79 percent by 2019, and increased further following pandemic-related spending.[11-01] These changes reflect both structural deficits and responses to economic shocks.

Drivers of Debt

Debt grows when expenditures exceed revenues. Major drivers include entitlement programs, discretionary spending, interest costs, and economic conditions. Social Security, Medicare, and Medicaid account for a large and growing share of federal spending. As the population ages, the number of beneficiaries increases relative to the number of workers, placing upward pressure on these programs.[11-03]

Revenue is influenced by economic growth, tax policy, and compliance. When growth slows or tax receipts decline, deficits can widen even if spending remains constant. Policy choices affecting tax rates and spending levels determine the long-term trajectory of debt.

Interest Costs and Compounding

Interest payments are a direct consequence of accumulated debt. As debt increases, so do interest obligations. In 2024, net interest payments exceeded $800 billion, making it one of the largest components of federal spending.[11-04]

Interest costs depend on both the level of debt and prevailing interest rates. When rates are low, debt can be financed at relatively modest cost. When rates rise, the cost of servicing existing and new debt increases. Because debt compounds over time, rising interest rates can accelerate the growth of total obligations even if primary deficits remain unchanged.

Debt Relative to Economic Capacity

Debt is often evaluated relative to the size of the economy. The debt-to-GDP ratio measures the capacity of an economy to support its debt. A larger economy can sustain a higher level of debt, while slower growth increases the relative burden.

Sustainability depends on the relationship between interest rates and economic growth. When the growth rate of the economy exceeds the interest rate on debt, the debt burden can stabilize or decline relative to GDP. When interest rates exceed growth, debt can increase as a share of the economy even without large primary deficits.

Long-Term Projections

Long-term projections indicate continued growth in federal debt under current policy. The Congressional Budget

Office projects that debt held by the public could exceed 150 percent of GDP within the next three decades if current spending and revenue patterns persist.[11-05]

These projections are driven primarily by rising costs in healthcare and retirement programs, along with increasing interest payments. Without adjustments to spending, revenue, or both, debt is expected to grow faster than the economy.

Economic Effects of Debt

Public debt can influence economic outcomes through several channels. Government borrowing affects interest rates, capital allocation, and investment. In some conditions, increased government borrowing can raise interest rates and reduce private investment, a phenomenon often described as crowding out.

In other conditions, particularly during periods of weak demand, government borrowing can support economic activity without significantly displacing private investment. The effect depends on broader economic conditions, including the level of savings and the stance of monetary policy.

High levels of debt can also affect expectations. If investors anticipate future tax increases or spending reductions, behavior may adjust accordingly. Confidence in fiscal stability influences borrowing costs and financial conditions.

Fiscal Flexibility

Debt affects the ability of government to respond to future shocks. Higher debt levels can limit fiscal flexibility by increasing interest costs and reducing available resources.

During economic crises, governments often expand spending to stabilize conditions. Elevated debt can constrain the scale or duration of such responses.

At the same time, the ability to borrow during crises can be critical. During the 2008 financial crisis and the COVID-19 pandemic, large-scale fiscal interventions were financed through increased borrowing. These actions supported incomes, stabilized financial systems, and mitigated deeper economic contraction.

Intergenerational Effects

Debt has implications across generations. Borrowing allows current spending to be financed without immediate taxation, shifting part of the cost to future taxpayers. The impact depends on how borrowed funds are used.

If borrowing supports productive investment that increases future output, future generations may benefit from higher income and capacity. If borrowing finances consumption without increasing productive capacity, future taxpayers may face higher burdens without corresponding gains.

The composition of spending therefore affects not only current outcomes but future economic conditions.

Global Position and Currency

The United States issues debt in its own currency and benefits from the role of the U.S. dollar as a global reserve currency. This position increases demand for U.S. Treasury securities and supports lower borrowing costs relative to many other countries.[11-06]

However, this position is not fixed. Sustained increases in debt, changes in global demand for dollar-denominated assets, or shifts in economic conditions could affect borrowing costs over time. The interaction between domestic fiscal policy and global financial markets influences the sustainability of debt.

Structural Balance and Adjustment

Fiscal sustainability requires maintaining a balance between spending, revenue, and economic growth so that debt remains stable relative to the economy. Adjustments can occur through changes in tax policy, spending levels, or growth rates.

Gradual adjustments can alter the trajectory of debt over time. Delayed adjustments can require more significant changes if imbalances persist. Policy decisions determine how and when these adjustments occur.

System Effects of Debt

Debt is not an isolated outcome. It reflects the operation of the broader system. Policy determines spending and revenue. Those choices affect deficits and debt. Debt influences interest costs, fiscal flexibility, and economic conditions. These outcomes feed back into policy decisions.

Over time, the accumulation of debt reflects repeated decisions within this system. As said previously, the path of debt is determined by how incentives influence spending, revenue, and economic behavior across cycles.

The direction is set by the interaction of these forces. When borrowing is aligned with growth and productive investment, debt can remain manageable. When borrowing persistently exceeds the capacity of the economy to support it, constraints increase.

Trade Policy

Trade policy determines how a nation engages with global markets, shaping the flow of goods, the structure of production, and the distribution of costs and benefits across the economy.

Tariffs

Tariffs are among the oldest policy tools used to influence trade, taxes on imports. Historically, tariffs were a primary source of federal revenue in the United States before the income tax was established in 1913. In the late 19th century, tariffs accounted for more than 50 percent of federal revenue.[11-01]

Today, tariffs serve a different role, protecting domestic industries, responding to foreign trade practices, and pursuing strategic objectives. When tariffs are imposed, they raise the cost of imported goods. In 2023, U.S. tariff revenue totaled approximately $80 billion.[11-02]

The economic effect of tariffs is direct, increasing prices for imported goods and often for domestic substitutes. Studies of the 2018–2019 U.S. tariffs found that most of the cost was passed on to U.S. consumers and firms through higher prices.[11-03] Tariffs on intermediate goods also raise production costs for domestic manufacturers, which can reduce competitiveness or lead to higher final prices.

Tariffs function as a consumption tax on imported goods. Because lower- and middle-income households spend a larger share of income on goods rather than services, tariffs tend to fall more heavily on those households. Research shows that recent U.S. tariffs had regressive effects, reducing real income proportionally more for lower-income groups.[11-04] Higher-income households, which spend more on services, are less affected.

Tariffs can also trigger responses. During recent trade disputes, U.S. exports faced retaliatory tariffs from trading partners. U.S. agricultural exports to China declined sharply after 2018 before partially recovering.[11-05] Over time, tariffs redistribute costs and benefits, protecting certain producers while increasing costs for consumers and downstream industries.

Trade Agreements

Trade agreements reduce barriers to trade between countries. These agreements address tariffs, quotas, regulatory standards, intellectual property, and dispute resolution. Major U.S. agreements include the United States–Mexico–Canada Agreement and agreements across multiple regions.

The scale of global trade is significant. U.S. trade in goods and services exceeded $7 trillion in 2023.[11-06] Trade supports millions of jobs, particularly in export-oriented industries such as manufacturing, agriculture, and services.

Trade agreements can lower costs and expand markets. Access to larger markets allows firms to scale production, while imports provide access to lower-cost goods and inputs. These effects can increase efficiency and raise overall economic output.

At the same time, trade agreements can produce uneven outcomes. Industries exposed to import competition may contract, while others expand. Research on the "China shock" found that increased import competition contributed to job losses in certain U.S. manufacturing regions, with lasting effects on employment and wages.[11-07]

These adjustments are not evenly distributed. Gains from trade are often broad but diffuse, while losses are concentrated in specific industries and regions. Policy responses influence how these effects are absorbed.

Import and Export Restrictions

Governments also influence trade through restrictions beyond tariffs. These include quotas, export controls, sanctions, and licensing requirements. These tools are often used for national security, foreign policy, or public safety objectives.

Export controls limit the transfer of sensitive technologies. In recent years, restrictions on advanced semiconductors have been used to limit access to strategic technologies. These controls affect global supply chains and investment decisions, particularly in high-technology sectors.[11-08]

Sanctions restrict trade with specific countries or entities. These measures can limit access to financial systems, technology, and goods. While sanctions can serve strategic objectives, they can also reduce trade volumes and affect global markets.

Quotas and licensing requirements can limit the quantity of goods traded. These restrictions can stabilize domestic industries or manage supply, but they can also reduce competition and increase prices.

These policies reflect that trade is not solely an economic issue. It is also tied to national security and geopolitical strategy. Decisions about which sectors remain open and which are restricted shape both economic and strategic capacity.

Industrial Policy

Industrial policy refers to government actions designed to influence the structure of the economy. This includes subsidies, tax incentives, public investment, and regulatory support aimed at specific industries.

Recent policy has focused on reshoring production in areas such as semiconductors, energy, and critical supply chains. The CHIPS and Science Act of 2022 provided more than $50 billion in incentives for domestic semiconductor manufacturing and research.[11-09] The Inflation Reduction Act included substantial incentives for domestic energy production and manufacturing.[11-10]

These policies reflect concerns about supply chain resilience and national security. Disruptions during the COVID-19 pandemic highlighted the risks of concentrated production in specific regions.

Industrial policy can encourage domestic investment and capacity. It can also shape where production occurs and which industries expand. However, it involves tradeoffs. Subsidies require public funding, and targeted support can favor certain industries over others. If poorly designed, industrial policy can lead to inefficiencies or misallocation of resources.

Global competition adds complexity. Many countries use industrial policy to support strategic industries, which can lead to subsidy competition and increased public cost.

Combined Effects

Tariffs, trade agreements, restrictions, and industrial policy interact to shape trade outcomes. These tools influence prices, production decisions, and the distribution of economic activity and also affect relationships with trading partners and the structure of global markets.

Trade policy is a set of choices about cost, risk, and capacity. Lower barriers can reduce costs but increase exposure to external shocks. Higher barriers can support domestic industries but raise prices and reduce competitiveness.

These choices also affect how costs are distributed. Tariffs and restrictions often raise consumer prices. Trade agreements can expand opportunity but concentrate adjustment costs. Industrial policy can support targeted sectors but requires public resources.

Over time, these decisions compound. If policy consistently prioritizes cost reduction and global efficiency, production tends to concentrate where costs are lowest, increasing exposure to disruption and shifting employment across regions. If policy emphasizes domestic capacity and resilience, costs may be higher, but supply chains may be more stable and responsive under stress.

Trade policy shapes how capital moves across borders, how production is organized, and how risk is distributed. Over long periods, it affects not only economic outcomes but national capacity and resilience.

At the same time, industrial policy involves tradeoffs. Targeted support can improve capacity in selected industries, but it may also distort markets, favor certain firms, and allocate resources based on policy priorities rather than market signals.

The effectiveness of industrial policy depends on design and implementation. Long-term success requires alignment between incentives, market conditions, and technological change. Poorly targeted policies can lead to inefficiency and misallocation of resources.

Combined Effects

Tariffs, trade agreements, restrictions, and industrial policy operate together to shape trade outcomes. These tools influence prices, production, and the allocation of resources across the economy.

Trade policy reflects choices about efficiency, security, and distribution. Open trade can reduce costs and increase efficiency but may expose the economy to external risks. Protective measures can support domestic industries and resilience but may increase costs and reduce competition.

These choices affect how capital is allocated and how production is organized, influencing which industries expand, where jobs are located, and how income is distributed across sectors and regions.

Over time, the effects of trade policy accumulate. Incentives shape investment, supply chains, and technological development. Small differences in policy can produce significant changes in economic structure.

Trade policy operates within a broader system that includes fiscal policy, monetary conditions, labor markets, and technological change. Outcomes reflect the combined effect of these forces.

Over long periods, trade policy influences not only economic performance but national capacity. Systems that balance efficiency with resilience can maintain both competitiveness and stability. Systems that prioritize one at the expense of the other may experience greater volatility or reduced flexibility as conditions change.

Section III — Capital and Market Conditions

Capital Formation and Access

Capital determines which ideas become businesses, which technologies are developed, and which jobs are created. It is the mechanism through which savings are transformed into production. The availability, cost, and distribution of capital shape economic outcomes across sectors and regions.

Capital Formation

Capital formation is the process by which resources are accumulated and directed toward investment. In the United States, this occurs through household savings, corporate retained earnings, government spending, and foreign investment.

The scale of capital formation is significant. Gross private domestic investment has averaged approximately 18 to 22 percent of GDP in recent years, representing more than $4 trillion annually.[11-01] Corporate profits have remained elevated, exceeding $3 trillion annually in recent years, providing substantial internal capital for reinvestment.[11-02]

Global capital flows further expand available investment. The total foreign direct investment position in the United States exceeds $5 trillion, reflecting its role as a primary destination for global capital.[11-03]

The constraint in modern economies is not the total supply of capital. It is how that capital is allocated.

Access to Capital

Access to capital is uneven. It is determined by creditworthiness, collateral, financial history, and access to networks. These factors influence both availability and cost.

Large firms have broad access to capital markets, issuing bonds, selling equity, and accessing institutional investors. In U.S. corporate bond markets, the majority of issuance is concentrated among large, investment-grade firms.[11-04]

Smaller firms face more limited options. Small businesses account for approximately 44 percent of U.S. GDP and about 46 percent of private sector employment yet rely heavily on bank lending and personal financing.[11-05]

Access disparities are reflected in approval rates. According to Federal Reserve surveys, large banks approve roughly 15 to 25 percent of small business loan applications, while large corporations routinely access public debt markets with far higher success rates.[11-06]

These differences affect who can enter markets, expand operations, and survive economic downturns.

Cost of Capital

The cost of capital determines whether investment is viable. It reflects interest rates, required returns, and perceived risk.

Interest rates directly affect borrowing costs. During the low-rate period of 2020–2021, U.S. corporations issued over $2 trillion in bonds in a single year, reflecting strong demand for financing at historically low rates.[11-07] As rates increased beginning in 2022, borrowing slowed and financing conditions tightened.

Cost differences vary across firms. Small business loan rates are often 2 to 6 percentage points higher than rates available to large corporations, reflecting higher perceived risk and limited access to capital markets.[11-08]

These differences compound over time. Lower-cost capital allows firms to invest more aggressively, acquire competitors, and expand market share. Higher-cost capital restricts growth and limits resilience.

Financial Intermediation

Capital is allocated through financial intermediaries, including banks, asset managers, private equity firms, and public markets. These institutions evaluate risk, structure transactions, and direct investment.

The scale of financial intermediation is large. Total U.S. financial assets exceed $120 trillion, with a substantial portion managed by institutional investors such as pension funds, mutual funds, and insurance companies.[11-09]

Private markets have expanded significantly. Global private equity assets under management have grown from approximately $1 trillion in 2000 to over $8 trillion in recent years.[11-10] Venture capital investment in the United States exceeded $200 billion at its peak in 2021.[11-11]

These intermediaries operate within incentive structures that influence allocation. Compensation models and performance metrics often emphasize short-term returns, which can favor investments with faster or more predictable payoffs.

Barriers to Entry

Capital requirements create barriers to entry. Industries such as manufacturing, energy, and technology often require substantial upfront investment. Regulatory compliance further increases costs.

Network effects and scale advantages reinforce these barriers. Established firms can leverage infrastructure, distribution networks, and customer bases, reducing marginal costs relative to new entrants.

These factors contribute to reduced competition. Research shows that "superstar firms" have captured a growing share of economic activity, with the top firms accounting for a disproportionate share of profits and market value.[11-12]

Concentration of Capital

Capital tends to flow toward firms with strong returns and lower perceived risk. This leads to concentration.

Market concentration has increased across many sectors. Concentration ratios indicate that the largest firms account for an increasing share of industry sales, with the top four firms exceeding 40 percent of market share in some industries.[11-13]

Large firms also hold a disproportionate share of assets. The largest 1 percent of firms account for a substantial portion of total corporate assets and revenues, reinforcing their access to capital markets.[11-14]

This concentration is self-reinforcing. Greater scale improves access to capital, which enables further expansion, acquisitions, and efficiency gains.

Geographic and Sector Allocation

Capital is unevenly distributed across regions and sectors. Investment tends to concentrate in areas with established infrastructure, skilled labor, and access to markets.

Venture capital investment is highly concentrated geographically. More than 70 percent of U.S. venture capital funding is directed to a small number of states, primarily California, New York, and Massachusetts.[11-15]

Sector concentration is also significant. Technology, healthcare, and financial services receive a disproportionate share of investment.

Regions with lower levels of investment often experience slower economic growth, fewer job opportunities, and lower income growth.

Public Policy and Capital Access

Public policy influences capital formation and access through taxation, regulation, monetary policy, and public investment. Monetary policy affects borrowing costs. Lower interest rates reduce the cost of capital and encourage borrowing. Higher rates increase costs and restrict access. Tax policy influences returns on investment. Corporate tax rates, capital gains taxes, and depreciation rules affect investment decisions.

Government programs can expand access to capital. The Small Business Administration supports tens of billions of dollars in lending annually through loan guarantees, reducing risk for lenders and increasing access for smaller firms.[11-16]

Regulation also shapes financial markets. Capital requirements, disclosure rules, and barriers to entry influence how capital is allocated and who can participate.

Implications for Economic Outcomes

Capital formation and access determine which firms are created, which industries expand, and which workers are employed, influencing wages, job availability, and economic mobility. When access to capital is broad, more participants can invest and compete. When access is concentrated, opportunities narrow, and economic outcomes diverge.

These patterns are the result of incentives, financial structures, and policy choices.

Transition to Allocation

Capital formation provides the supply of investment. Access determines who can participate. The next step is allocation, where decisions are made about how capital is deployed across the economy.

Allocation determines which firms grow, which technologies are adopted, and how work is structured.

Capital Mobility

Capital moves. It moves across firms, sectors, and borders in response to incentives, risk, regulation, and expected return. This mobility is a defining feature of modern economic systems. It determines where production occurs, where jobs are created, and how value is distributed.

Capital is not bound by geography in the same way as labor. Advances in financial markets, technology, and trade have reduced the friction associated with moving capital. As a result, investment decisions can be made across jurisdictions with relative ease. This creates both opportunity and pressure. Regions compete for capital, and capital responds to those conditions.

Domestic vs Offshore Investment

Investment decisions are influenced by differences in cost, regulation, taxation, and market access. Firms allocate capital between domestic and offshore locations based on expected returns after accounting for these factors.

Foreign direct investment reflects these decisions. U.S. multinational firms hold trillions of dollars in assets abroad, while foreign firms invest heavily in the United States. The outward direct investment position of U.S. firms exceeds $6 trillion, while inward foreign direct investment in the United States exceeds $5 trillion.[12-01,12-02] These flows represent long-term commitments to production, facilities, and operations.

Cost differences are a primary driver. Labor costs, regulatory compliance, and tax rates vary across countries. Firms may locate production where costs are lower or where supply chains are more efficient. Market access also matters.

Firms often invest within a region to serve that market directly, avoiding tariffs and reducing transportation costs.

Tax policy influences location decisions. Differences in corporate tax rates, treatment of foreign earnings, and transfer pricing rules affect after-tax returns. Changes in tax policy can shift incentives and alter investment patterns.

Domestic investment is influenced by similar factors. Regions within a country compete for capital through tax incentives, infrastructure, and workforce availability. Investment flows toward areas with favorable conditions, leading to regional differences in growth and employment.

Capital Flight

Capital flight occurs when assets are moved out of a country in response to perceived risk. This can include political instability, regulatory changes, currency risk, or concerns about expropriation. Capital flight can take the form of portfolio investment, direct investment, or movement of financial assets.

Global financial markets allow capital to move quickly. Cross-border portfolio flows can shift in response to changes in interest rates, inflation expectations, or political developments. During periods of uncertainty, investors may move capital to jurisdictions perceived as more stable.

Emerging markets are particularly sensitive to capital flight. Changes in global interest rates can lead to outflows, affecting exchange rates and financial conditions. In 2022, rising interest rates in advanced economies contributed to significant capital outflows from emerging markets, increasing borrowing costs and currency volatility.[12-03]

Capital flight can have significant effects on domestic economies. Reduced investment can slow growth, limit job creation, and weaken financial systems. Currency depreciation can increase the cost of imports and external debt. Governments may respond with capital controls, but these can introduce additional distortions.

Supply Chain Relocation

Capital mobility is reflected in the location of production. Firms allocate capital to build facilities, develop supply chains, and organize production across regions. These decisions determine where goods are produced and how they move through the global economy.

Global supply chains have expanded over several decades, driven by cost efficiencies and technological advances. Firms have located production in regions with lower costs or specialized capabilities. Manufacturing capacity has shifted toward countries with lower labor costs and strong export infrastructure.

These patterns are not fixed. Supply chains adjust in response to changing conditions. Trade policy, geopolitical risk, and disruptions can lead firms to relocate production. The COVID-19 pandemic exposed vulnerabilities in global supply chains, leading to reassessment of sourcing strategies and increased emphasis on resilience.

Relocation can take several forms. Firms may reshore production to domestic markets, nearshore to neighboring countries, or diversify suppliers across multiple regions. These decisions involve tradeoffs between cost, risk, and reliability.

Changes in supply chains affect employment and regional development. Shifts in production can lead to job losses in one region and gains in another. Over time, these changes reshape industrial structure and economic geography.

Cross-Border Investment

Cross-border investment includes both direct investment in physical assets and portfolio investment in financial instruments. These flows connect economies and allow capital to be allocated globally.

Portfolio investment is large and liquid. Global equity and bond markets facilitate investment across countries. Total global financial assets exceed $400 trillion, and cross-border holdings represent a significant share of these assets.[12-04] Investors allocate capital based on expected returns, diversification, and risk.

Direct investment involves longer-term commitments. It includes building facilities, acquiring companies, and establishing operations in foreign markets. These investments are less liquid but can provide access to new markets, resources, and capabilities.

Cross-border investment can support economic growth. It provides capital for development, transfers technology, and integrates economies. However, it also introduces exposure to global financial conditions. Changes in interest rates, exchange rates, or investor sentiment can affect capital flows.

Regulation influences cross-border investment. Countries may impose restrictions on foreign ownership, require approvals for certain transactions, or implement screening mechanisms for national security reasons. These policies affect the flow of capital and the structure of investment.

Capital mobility is therefore shaped by a combination of market forces and policy choices. The movement of capital across borders reflects differences in incentives, risk, and opportunity.

Implications for Allocation

Capital mobility affects how capital is allocated across the global economy. It determines where investment occurs, which industries expand, and how production is organized.

When capital moves freely, it seeks the highest risk-adjusted return. This can increase efficiency but also create disparities between regions. Areas that attract capital grow more rapidly, while others may experience reduced investment.

Policy can influence these outcomes. Tax policy, regulation, and trade agreements affect incentives for capital movement. Changes in these policies can alter investment patterns and reshape economic structure.

Understanding capital mobility is essential to understanding allocation. The movement of capital sets the stage for decisions about where and how resources are deployed. Those decisions determine the structure of production, the availability of jobs, and the distribution of income.

Market Power and Barriers to Entry

Market outcomes reflect not only supply and demand but also competition and the distribution of power within the market. Market power influences pricing, wages, investment, and resource allocation, while barriers to entry determine who can participate. When barriers are high, fewer firms compete and market power increases. Over time this can lead to concentration, where a small number of firms control a large share of economic activity.

Market Competition and Concentration

Competition depends on how many firms operate in a market and how they compete. In competitive markets, many firms participate, and no single firm can influence price. In concentrated markets, a small number of firms dominate, and pricing power increases. Concentration has increased across many sectors of the U.S. economy. Measures such as concentration ratios and the Herfindahl-Hirschman Index show that the largest firms account for a growing share of revenue in industries including technology, healthcare, finance, and retail.[13-01]

The rise of "superstar firms" illustrates this trend. A small number of highly productive firms capture a disproportionate share of sales, profits, and market value. Research shows that these firms account for a significant portion of the decline in labor's share of income, reflecting both increased productivity and increased market power.[13-02]

Concentration can result from efficiency. Larger firms may achieve economies of scale, reduce costs, and improve productivity. However, concentration can also reduce competition. With fewer competitors, firms may have greater ability to influence prices, limit output, and shape market conditions.

Pricing Power

Market power allows firms to influence prices. In competitive markets, prices are driven toward marginal cost. In concentrated markets, firms may be able to charge prices above cost, increasing margins.

Evidence of pricing power can be seen in markups. Studies indicate that average markups have increased over recent decades, suggesting that firms are able to price above competitive levels.[13-03] Higher markups can increase profitability but may also reduce consumer surplus.

Pricing power is not uniform. It varies across industries and firms. Companies with strong brands, differentiated products, or limited competition may have greater pricing flexibility. In contrast, firms in highly competitive markets may have little ability to raise prices.

Pricing decisions affect consumers directly. Higher prices reduce purchasing power. Over time, this can affect demand, consumption patterns, and economic welfare.

Barriers to Entry

Barriers to entry are conditions that make it difficult for new firms to enter a market. These barriers can be structural, regulatory, financial, or strategic.

Capital requirements are a primary barrier. Industries such as manufacturing, energy, and technology often require significant upfront investment. New firms must secure capital before they can compete.

Regulation can also create barriers. Licensing requirements, compliance costs, and approval processes can limit entry. While regulation can protect consumers and ensure standards, it can also increase costs and reduce competition.

Economies of scale create additional barriers. Larger firms can spread fixed costs over greater output, reducing per-unit cost. This advantage can make it difficult for smaller firms to compete on price.

Network effects can reinforce barriers. In markets where value increases with the number of users, such as digital platforms, established firms can become dominant. New entrants may struggle to attract users without an existing network.

Access to distribution channels is another barrier. Established firms often control relationships with suppliers, retailers, or customers. These relationships can limit the ability of new firms to reach the market.

Strategic Barriers

Firms can create barriers intentionally. Strategic behavior can limit competition and protect market position.

Pricing strategies can be used to deter entry. Incumbent firms may reduce prices temporarily to make entry less attractive. While this may benefit consumers in the short term, it can discourage new competitors.

Control of inputs can also be used to limit competition. Firms that control key resources, technology, or intellectual property may restrict access, preventing others from entering the market.

Mergers and acquisitions can increase concentration. Firms may acquire potential competitors or complementary businesses, expanding market share and reducing competition. In the United States, merger activity has remained high, with thousands of transactions annually.[13-04]

These strategies can reinforce market power. Over time, they can reduce the number of competitors and increase barriers to entry.

Labor Market Power

Market power is not limited to product markets. It also exists in labor markets. When a small number of employers dominate a local labor market, they may have greater influence over wages and working conditions.

This form of power is often referred to as monopsony. In concentrated labor markets, workers may have fewer employment options, reducing their bargaining power. Research indicates that labor market concentration is associated with lower wages, particularly in less competitive regions.[13-05]

Restrictions on worker mobility can reinforce this effect. Non-compete agreements, occupational licensing, and limited job availability can reduce worker options. When workers cannot easily change employers, wage competition is reduced.

Labor market power affects income distribution. Lower wages reduce household income and limit economic mobility.

Innovation and Entry

Barriers to entry affect innovation. New firms often introduce new products, technologies, and business models. When entry is limited, the pace of innovation may slow.

Large firms can invest in research and development, but they may also have incentives to protect existing business models. In some cases, dominant firms acquire smaller, innovative firms, integrating their technology while reducing independent competition.

The relationship between concentration and innovation is complex. Scale can support investment, but reduced competition can limit the incentive to innovate.

Policy and Enforcement

Public policy influences market power and barriers to entry. Antitrust laws are designed to prevent anti-competitive behavior, promote competition, and protect consumers.

In the United States, enforcement is carried out by agencies such as the Department of Justice and the Federal Trade Commission. These agencies review mergers, investigate anti-competitive conduct, and enforce competition laws.

Policy decisions affect how markets evolve. Changes in enforcement priorities can alter the level of competition. Stricter enforcement can limit concentration, while weaker enforcement may allow greater consolidation.

Regulation can also influence entry. Policies that reduce unnecessary barriers can support competition, while policies that increase compliance costs can limit entry.

Implications for Economic Outcomes

Market power and barriers to entry shape economic outcomes, determining pricing, wages, investment, and participation, and influencing which firms compete, which survive, and how value is distributed.

Barriers

When competition is strong and barriers are low, firms must compete on price, quality, and innovation. Entry is possible, allowing new firms to challenge incumbents and offer alternatives to consumers. This competitive pressure forces firms to improve performance and allocate resources efficiently.

When barriers are high and markets are concentrated, outcomes change. Pricing power increases, entry declines, and innovation may slow. Wages can be constrained where employers have greater control, and concentration begins to shape outcomes more than competition.[14-01,14-04]

These conditions result from the interaction of incentives, competition, and policy. Changes in technology, regulation, or economic conditions can alter both market power and barriers to entry, shifting how resources are allocated.

Understanding these dynamics is essential to understanding how economic systems produce outcomes.

Antitrust

Antitrust law addresses how economic power is formed, exercised, and limited. It focuses on whether markets remain competitive or whether power becomes entrenched. The objective is not only to prevent monopolies but to preserve the conditions under which competition can occur.

Antitrust is no longer limited to traditional measures such as market share. In digital markets, power can arise from control of data, platforms, and access to users. These forms of control can create barriers that are not captured by conventional metrics but can still restrict competition.

The purpose of antitrust is to maintain competitive conditions by preventing monopolization, restricting anti-competitive practices, and limiting mergers that reduce competition.[14-11] Enforcement therefore plays a direct role in shaping competition and access.

Antitrust enforcement has changed over time. In earlier decades, enforcement was more frequent, particularly against large firms. In the 1960s and 1970s, the Department of Justice brought roughly 20 major cases per year against large corporations, declining to fewer than 10 per year after the 1980s.[14-15] At the same time, merger activity has remained high, with more than 2,000 transactions reported annually in recent years, while only a small fraction are challenged.[14-16] In some recent years, enforcement actions have been at their lowest levels relative to transaction volume, suggesting that enforcement has not kept pace with the scale and complexity of modern markets.[14-17]

According to Robert Reich, five corporations control approximately 90 percent of the U.S. media market, the number of major airlines has declined from twelve carriers in 1980 to four today, and four firms control about 80 percent of meat processing.[14-20] These patterns reflect a broader trend toward consolidation across multiple industries.

Enforcement outcomes depend on how competition is defined. A narrow focus on price may allow concentration if prices remain stable. A broader approach considers competition, barriers to entry, innovation, and long-term effects, leading to different conclusions about market power.[14-06]

Competition

Competition functions as a structural constraint on power. It limits pricing, forces efficiency, and creates incentives for innovation. Firms must respond to alternatives or risk losing market share.

When competition is present, successful products attract imitation. New firms enter, attempt to improve on existing offerings, and compete for customers. This process can lower prices, improve quality, and expand consumer choice over time.

When competition is limited, this process weakens. Firms face less pressure to improve or reduce costs, and outcomes become more dependent on concentration. Reduced entry allows incumbents to maintain position and influence over pricing and output.

Competition also affects capital allocation. Capital flows toward firms that can grow and compete, reinforcing successful business models. When entry is restricted, capital concentrates in existing firms, strengthening their position and limiting new competition.[14-13]

International Competition

Competition operates across borders as well as within domestic markets. Firms compete globally, and differences in policy, regulation, and cost structure influence how that competition unfolds. These differences can act as either advantages or barriers.

Countries adopt different approaches to competition. Some emphasize open competition with limited intervention, while others actively shape markets through regulation, subsidies, or industrial policy. These choices affect how firms compete and where investment flows.

Restrictions on foreign firms, data requirements, and regulatory standards can function as barriers to entry. At the same time, subsidies and state support can strengthen domestic firms in global markets. These policies can alter competitive balance without directly affecting prices.

The European Union has adopted a more interventionist approach in digital markets, focusing on concentration and long-term competition. Regulations such as the Digital Markets Act are designed to limit the dominance of large platform firms and ensure access for competitors.[14-08] The United States has traditionally emphasized competition through market forces, with antitrust focused more narrowly on consumer outcomes.

Equal Opportunities for Businesses

Access to markets determines who can compete. Even when formal barriers are limited, structural conditions can restrict participation. These conditions shape whether competition is open or constrained.

Supply chain control is one mechanism. Firms with established supplier relationships, distribution networks, or purchasing scale can secure preferential access. This can limit the ability of smaller firms to compete, even when their products are competitive.

Economies of scale create additional advantages. Larger firms can reduce unit costs, invest in technology, and absorb short-term losses. These advantages can deter entry and reinforce existing market positions.

Policies that affect access to suppliers, distribution, and financing influence competition. When access is broad, firms compete on performance. When access is limited, competition shifts toward control of inputs and channels rather than quality or efficiency.

Fair Competition

Antitrust enforcement reflects how competition is defined and protected. Laws such as the Sherman Act and the Clayton Act established the framework for preventing monopolization and anti-competitive conduct. These laws provide the basis for evaluating market behavior and structure.

Enforcement varies over time. Changes in legal standards, agency resources, and policy priorities affect how aggressively competition is protected. This can lead to periods of stronger or weaker enforcement.

Debate continues over whether enforcement has kept pace with rising concentration. In digital markets, network effects, data control, and platform dominance create forms of power that differ from traditional industrial markets. These differences complicate the application of existing frameworks.

Some argue that current enforcement is insufficient to address concentration, particularly in technology and communications. Others argue that excessive intervention may reduce innovation and weaken firms in global competition. Antitrust policy therefore reflects a balance between limiting concentration and preserving incentives for growth.

European Union Enforcement

The European Union has taken an active role in regulating large technology firms. Enforcement actions have focused on market dominance, access to platforms, and control of data. These actions are intended to address structural barriers to competition.

Major firms have faced fines and restrictions related to search, advertising, and app distribution. Regulators have sought to limit practices that restrict access and to maintain competitive conditions within digital markets.

Regulatory scrutiny has also focused on acquisitions and data practices. Authorities have examined whether acquisitions reduce future competition and whether control of data creates barriers to entry. These concerns reflect broader questions about competition and concentration.

This approach emphasizes long-term competition and market openness. Differences between U.S. and EU approaches highlight broader questions about regulation, innovation, and the role of government in shaping markets.

Patented Monopoly

Patents create temporary exclusivity intended to support innovation. By granting a limited period of protection, they allow firms to recover development costs and invest in new technologies. This exclusivity is a form of market power.

At the same time, patents restrict competition during the period of protection. Firms holding patents can set prices without direct competition, which can affect access and pricing.

The U.S. patent system has evolved over time through legislative and administrative changes designed to balance innovation and competition.[14-10] The effectiveness of this balance depends on how patents are defined, granted, and enforced.

When exclusivity is limited and targeted, patents can encourage investment. When it is broad or extended, it can create barriers to entry and limit competition.

U.S. Antitrust Enforcement

Recent enforcement actions reflect increased attention to market concentration across multiple industries. Investigations have focused on technology, healthcare, finance, and other sectors where market power may affect competition.

Regulators examine mergers, platform control, pricing practices, and data use to determine whether these activities limit competition. These reviews are intended to prevent consolidation that could reduce market access.

Merger activity remains high, with thousands of transactions annually, increasing the importance of effective review.[14-12] Enforcement actions can prevent consolidation, require divestitures, or impose conditions on business practices.[14-07]

The effectiveness of enforcement depends on timing, resources, and legal standards. Complex markets and long development cycles can make it difficult to identify and address anti-competitive behavior before it becomes entrenched.

Market Regulation

The role of regulation in markets is debated. One perspective favors minimal intervention, emphasizing the role of competition and market forces. Another supports stronger oversight to limit concentration and preserve competition.

In digital markets, these issues are more pronounced. Large firms can control platforms, data, and distribution, creating new forms of market power that are not easily addressed by traditional frameworks.

Regulation can address these conditions by limiting certain practices, increasing transparency, or requiring access for competitors. However, regulation can also increase complexity and introduce new barriers.

The challenge is to balance flexibility with control. Too little regulation can allow concentration to increase, while too much regulation can limit entry and slow innovation.

Price Dynamics and Market Power

Pricing reflects both cost and the level of competition. In competitive markets, prices tend to reflect cost and efficiency. In concentrated markets, pricing can reflect market power.

Evidence indicates that average markups have increased over recent decades, suggesting that firms are able to price above competitive levels.[14-03] This reflects increased ability to influence prices in certain sectors.

Advances in data and automation have made pricing more dynamic. Firms can adjust prices quickly in response to cost, demand, and competitive conditions. This can improve efficiency but also increases the importance of competition.

Consumers often have limited information and limited ability to respond. When competition is limited, pricing strategies can have a greater impact on outcomes, affecting how value is distributed.

Labor Market Effects

Market power extends to labor markets. When a small number of employers dominate a labor market, workers have fewer options. This reduces bargaining power and can affect wages and working conditions.

Research shows that labor market concentration is associated with lower wages, particularly in less competitive regions.[14-05] Limited mobility and fewer alternatives reduce the ability of workers to negotiate.

The rise of large, highly productive firms has also been associated with a declining share of income going to labor. This reflects shifts in bargaining power and increasing concentration.[14-02]

Implications for the System

Market power and barriers to entry shape the economy, determining who participates, how competition functions, and how value is distributed. When entry is possible and competition is strong, outcomes are shaped by performance. When entry is limited and markets are concentrated, outcomes are shaped by structure rather than competition.

These conditions affect capital allocation, job creation, wages, and innovation, influencing the distribution of opportunity and the stability of the system. Market outcomes result from the interaction of incentives, market design, and policy. Understanding this interaction is necessary to understand how economic systems produce results.

Ownership and Control Structures

Ownership determines who holds claims on assets. Control determines who makes decisions about how those assets are used. In many cases, ownership and control are aligned. In others, ownership and control are separate. This separation is a defining feature of modern economic systems and affects how decisions are made and how outcomes are produced. The structure of ownership and control influences incentives. It affects risk, time horizon, and accountability. These factors shape how firms allocate capital, manage operations, and respond to competition.

Separation of Ownership and Control

In large corporations, ownership is typically dispersed among shareholders, while control is exercised by management. In the United States, institutional investors hold the majority of public equity, and the largest asset managers hold significant stakes across a wide range of firms. The three largest asset managers, BlackRock, Vanguard, and State Street, together hold substantial ownership positions in a large share of S&P 500 companies.[15-01,15-02]

This separation creates an agency relationship, where managers act on behalf of owners. Agency relationships introduce potential conflicts. Managers may pursue objectives that differ from those of shareholders, including growth, compensation, or risk avoidance.

Corporate governance mechanisms are designed to align these interests. Boards of directors oversee management, approve major decisions, and represent shareholder interests. Shareholder voting provides another mechanism for influence, although participation and coordination vary across firms.

The separation of ownership and control allows firms to scale by raising capital from a broad base of investors while centralizing decision-making. However, it also reduces direct accountability between owners and decision-makers.

Concentrated Ownership

Not all firms have dispersed ownership. In many cases, ownership is concentrated in the hands of founders, families, or large investors. Globally, a significant share of large firms remain family-controlled, particularly outside the United States, where concentrated ownership structures are more common.[15-03]

Private equity represents another form of concentrated ownership. Private equity firms acquire companies using a combination of equity and debt and often take an active role in management. Global private equity assets under management have grown to more than $10 trillion, reflecting the increasing role of concentrated ownership structures in corporate control.[15-04]

Concentrated ownership can strengthen control and support long-term decision-making. Founder-led firms often retain significant ownership stakes, which can align decision-making with long-term objectives. However, concentrated ownership can also reduce oversight and limit minority shareholder influence.

Institutional Ownership

Institutional investors, including pension funds, mutual funds, and asset managers, hold a large share of equity in public markets. In the United States, institutional ownership of public equities has risen from roughly 20 percent in the 1950s to over 70 percent today.[15-05]

A small number of large asset managers control a significant portion of these holdings. The largest firms often hold diversified stakes across competing companies within the same industry, raising questions about influence, governance, and competition.[15-02]

Institutional investors can influence corporate behavior through voting, engagement, and governance practices. However, they also introduce additional layers of agency, as asset managers act on behalf of underlying investors. Incentives may be influenced by short-term performance metrics and portfolio considerations.

The concentration of ownership among institutional investors has increased the scale of influence while also diffusing direct accountability.

Control Through Financial Structure

Control is not determined by equity ownership alone. Financial structure also affects decision-making. Debt holders, creditors, and other stakeholders can influence corporate behavior.

Corporate debt levels have increased over time. U.S. nonfinancial corporate debt has exceeded $13 trillion in recent years, increasing the importance of debt in shaping corporate decisions.[15-06]

Debt imposes obligations that constrain decision-making. Firms must meet interest and principal payments, which can limit flexibility and increase sensitivity to cash flow. In highly leveraged firms, these constraints can influence investment, hiring, and operational decisions.

In periods of financial distress, control can shift from equity holders to creditors. Debt covenants and restructuring processes can give creditors significant influence over strategy, management, and asset allocation.

Financial structure therefore affects both incentives and control, shaping risk, flexibility, and decision-making authority.

Dual-Class Shares and Voting Control

Some firms use dual-class share structures, where different classes of shares carry different voting rights. This allows founders or insiders to retain control while raising capital from public investors.

Dual-class structures are common among technology firms and have become more prevalent in public offerings. A growing share of IPOs in the United States include dual-class share structures, allowing founders to retain voting control despite holding a minority of economic ownership.[15-07]

These structures can support long-term decision-making by insulating management from short-term market pressures. However, they also reduce the influence of other shareholders and can limit accountability.

The distribution of voting power, rather than ownership alone, determines who controls the firm. This separation can persist even as ownership becomes more dispersed.

Control Without Ownership

Control can also be exercised without significant ownership. Management teams, boards, and controlling stakeholders can influence decisions through position rather than equity.

In widely held firms, management may have substantial autonomy. Dispersed shareholders may lack the coordination needed to influence decisions, allowing managers to exercise control without large ownership stakes.

Control can also arise through contractual arrangements, partnerships, or control of key assets. Firms that control distribution channels, data, or platforms can exert influence over other participants in the market.

In digital markets, control of data and user networks has become a significant source of power. Firms that control these assets can influence access, pricing, and competitive dynamics even without traditional ownership structures.

Implications for Decision-Making

Ownership and control shape how decisions are made, influencing time horizons, risk tolerance, and strategic priorities. Firms with dispersed ownership often focus on financial performance and market expectations. Firms with concentrated ownership may prioritize long-term growth or control. Financial structure can shift focus toward cash flow, debt obligations, and risk management.

These differences affect investment, employment, and competition. Control shapes how firms respond to opportunities and constraints. Ownership and control also affect accountability. When aligned, decision-makers bear more direct consequences. When separate, governance mechanisms align incentives and monitor behavior.

Implications for Economic Outcomes

Ownership and control structures influence how value is created and distributed, affecting who benefits from economic activity and how decisions impact workers, consumers, and investors. Concentration of control can reinforce market power. Firms with strong control positions may be better able to maintain barriers to entry, influence pricing, or shape market conditions. This can affect competition and the allocation of resources.

At the same time, effective control can support investment and innovation. Clear decision-making authority can enable firms to pursue long-term strategies and allocate capital efficiently. The balance between ownership, control, and accountability shapes economic outcomes. It determines how power is exercised within firms and how those firms interact within the broader economy.

Global Trade and Strategic Capacity

Financial systems, corporate organization, and taxation are closely tied to how work is organized. These systems determine where capital flows, which industries expand, and how employment is created, compensated, or eliminated.

Domestic vs global production balance

Economic self-sufficiency has reemerged as a strategic concern as global supply chains have proven vulnerable to disruption, conflict, and political leverage. Dependence on foreign production for critical goods, including energy infrastructure, advanced technology, pharmaceuticals, rare earth elements, and key materials, exposes the nation to economic pressure and limits flexibility during crises, including military conflict or geopolitical escalation.

Encouraging the return or preservation of domestic manufacturing capacity can be supported through advances in artificial intelligence, automation, robotics, and advanced machine tooling. These technologies reduce the labor cost differential that has historically driven offshoring decisions. Protecting intellectual property is equally critical, as the transfer of technology without adequate safeguards can weaken long-term competitiveness and erode strategic capacity.

Recent policy actions reflect these concerns. The United States has imposed tariffs on certain industrial goods and enacted targeted support for domestic semiconductor production through legislation such as the CHIPS and

Science Act. Federal incentives for semiconductor manufacturing exceed $50 billion, aimed at increasing domestic capacity in an industry that underpins defense, communications, and advanced computing.[16-01] When production is concentrated outside national jurisdiction, strategic leverage diminishes. When domestic capacity is maintained, flexibility during disruption is preserved.

At the same time, complete economic self-sufficiency is neither realistic nor economically efficient. Trade allows specialization, lowers costs, and supports innovation. The central issue is not whether to trade, but where vulnerability becomes dependency and where resilience justifies domestic capacity.

Competing Economic Frameworks

Economic policy reflects competing views about the role of markets and government. The Chicago School emphasizes market efficiency, price signals, limited regulation, and monetary discipline. It holds that decentralized markets allocate resources more effectively than centralized control and that excessive intervention distorts incentives.

Keynesian economics places greater emphasis on government intervention to stabilize economic cycles. During downturns, increased public spending and accommodative policy are used to prevent prolonged recession. During expansionary periods, fiscal restraint and tighter monetary policy are intended to contain inflation.

Modern economic governance incorporates elements of both approaches. Market mechanisms dominate routine allocation decisions, while intervention often occurs during systemic stress. The debate is less about ideology than about timing, scale, accountability, and measurable outcomes.

Global Trends and Economic Complexity

Recent decades have exposed the limits of simplified economic models. Globalization, digital platforms, supply-chain integration, pandemic disruption, geopolitical conflict, and technological acceleration have revealed how interconnected systems amplify both opportunity and risk.

Markets can self-correct in many areas. Innovation displaces outdated industries, and capital reallocates toward higher returns. However, certain disruptions, including financial contagion, pandemic shutdowns, and war-related supply shocks, expose vulnerabilities that markets alone do not immediately resolve.

Economic systems now operate in an environment of persistent complexity. Adaptive policy requires flexibility without abandoning discipline. The objective is not constant intervention, but calibrated response when systemic risk threatens broader stability or national resilience.

Borders, Labor, and Economic Incentives

Border policy is often framed as a security issue, but it is also an economic issue. Migration flows respond to wage differentials, labor demand, and economic opportunity. When income disparities between countries are large, enforcement alone cannot eliminate migration pressure.

The scale of the challenge underscores this reality. The United States manages more than 7,400 miles of land, lake, and river borders, along with over 11,000 miles of coastline.[16-02] Sustained physical enforcement across such distances is costly and imperfect, while economic incentives operate continuously and at scale.

Long-term migration patterns are shaped by labor demand within the United States and economic conditions abroad. Strengthening economic opportunity in neighboring regions can reduce outward migration pressure more effectively than enforcement alone. Trade relationships, development strategies, investment flows, and labor market conditions all influence migration patterns.

Viewed through an economic lens, border challenges reflect structural imbalances in opportunity rather than solely enforcement limitations.

The 2007–2008 Financial Crisis

The financial crisis shows how decisions within financial markets can reshape the entire system. Prior to the crisis, housing expansion, credit growth, and complex financial instruments created an appearance of stability. Market participants relied on assumptions of continuous asset appreciation and risk dispersion.

When housing prices declined and leveraged financial instruments unraveled, the consequences extended beyond financial firms. U.S. household net worth declined by more than $13 trillion between 2007 and 2009, and unemployment rose above 10 percent.[16-03] These effects spread across employment, credit availability, and public finances.

Government intervention followed, including emergency stabilization measures and subsequent reforms. Congress enacted the Dodd-Frank Wall Street Reform and Consumer Protection Act in 2010 to increase oversight, strengthen capital requirements, and improve consumer protections. Internationally, the Basel III framework raised capital and liquidity standards to improve resilience and reduce systemic risk.

Although Dodd-Frank remains in effect, subsequent legislation in 2018 adjusted its regulatory framework, easing requirements for certain financial institutions while leaving its core structure intact. The episode demonstrates how economic policy decisions have lasting structural consequences and how oversight requires continual reassessment rather than one-time reform.

The crisis revealed that economic frameworks must account not only for efficiency and growth, but also for systemic fragility.

Inflation and Policy Tradeoffs

Inflation is widely disliked because of its broad effects. It reduces purchasing power, creates uncertainty, and disproportionately affects fixed-income households. It also distorts price signals, raises interest rates, erodes savings, and can weaken long-term investment.

Recent inflation illustrates these effects. Consumer prices in the United States rose by more than 9 percent year-over-year in mid-2022, the highest rate in four decades, before moderating following monetary tightening.[16-04] Rapid increases in prices affect consumption, savings, and investment decisions across the economy.

Inflationary periods can also enable pricing practices that raise concerns about transparency, including shrinkflation, delayed price reductions, and complex fee structures. These practices can shift costs to consumers in ways that are not immediately visible.

Policy responses to inflation involve tradeoffs. Monetary tightening can reduce inflation but may slow growth and increase unemployment. Fiscal stimulus can support demand but may contribute to price pressures. Managing inflation requires balancing these competing effects across time.

Rule of Law and Economic Integration

Economic activity increasingly crosses national borders. Capital, labor, information, and goods move faster than traditional enforcement systems can manage. As markets integrate, legal coordination becomes an economic requirement.

Contract enforcement, property rights, trade standards, and intellectual property protections reduce uncertainty and encourage investment. International agreements establish baseline expectations, even though enforcement varies across jurisdictions.

Global trade has expanded significantly over time. World exports of goods and services have grown from less than 15 percent of global GDP in 1970 to more than 30 percent in recent years, reflecting increased economic integration.[16-05] This integration increases both opportunity and exposure to external shocks.

Cybersecurity, cross-border financial crime, supply-chain integrity, environmental risk, and digital commerce illustrate how legal coordination functions as economic infrastructure. These frameworks shape incentives, allocate risk, and influence how authority operates within and between nations.

A fully unified global legal system remains unlikely. However, targeted cooperation has proven feasible where mutual economic interest exists. In an interconnected world, the rule of law is not only a domestic safeguard but also a component of economic competitiveness.

Economic options are structural decisions about resilience, dependency, stability, and the distribution of risk. Markets generate growth and innovation, but they also concentrate power and transmit shocks. Government intervention can stabilize systems, but poorly designed policy can distort incentives and weaken growth.

The enduring challenge is not choosing between markets and government. It is designing an economic framework in which power remains accountable, vulnerability is reduced, resilience is strengthened, and growth remains sustainable within constitutional limits.

These choices are carried out through administrative structures that translate policy into action.

Domestic vs Global Production Capacity

The balance between domestic and global production reflects tradeoffs between efficiency and resilience. Global production allows firms to reduce costs by locating production where labor, materials, or regulatory conditions are most favorable. Domestic production provides greater control, security, and responsiveness during disruption.

Over recent decades, a substantial share of manufacturing capacity shifted offshore. In the United States, manufacturing employment declined from approximately 17 million workers in 2000 to about 12 million in recent years, reflecting both offshoring and automation.[16-06] While productivity increased, domestic capacity in certain sectors diminished.

Recent disruptions have highlighted the risks of concentration. Shortages of semiconductors, medical supplies, and critical components during the COVID-19 pandemic exposed the vulnerability of extended supply chains. Lead times increased, production slowed, and downstream industries were affected.

Policy responses have focused on rebuilding capacity in strategic sectors. Incentives for domestic semiconductor production, energy independence, and supply chain diversification reflect an effort to reduce reliance on single sources or regions. These efforts do not eliminate global production but seek to balance efficiency with resilience.

The appropriate balance depends on the nature of the industry. For non-critical goods, global sourcing may remain efficient. For essential goods, including defense, energy, and advanced technology, domestic or diversified capacity may be necessary to maintain stability.

The allocation of production is therefore not purely an economic decision. It reflects strategic considerations about risk, control, and long-term capacity.

Inflation and Monetary Policy

Monetary policy directly affects economic incentives through interest rates, credit conditions, and expectations. Changes in policy influence borrowing, investment, consumption, and asset prices.

A recent case illustrates these effects. In response to elevated inflation, the Federal Reserve increased the federal funds rate from near zero in early 2022 to over 5 percent by 2023.16-07 This rapid increase raised borrowing costs across the economy.

Higher interest rates reduced demand in interest-sensitive sectors. Mortgage rates more than doubled, contributing to a decline in housing affordability and a slowdown in home sales. Business investment also adjusted as the cost of capital increased.

At the same time, higher rates increased returns on savings and reduced inflationary pressure over time. Price growth moderated as demand cooled and financial conditions tightened.

These changes illustrate how monetary policy alters incentives. Lower rates encourage borrowing and investment but can contribute to inflation. Higher rates restrain demand and stabilize prices but can slow growth and increase unemployment.

Monetary policy therefore involves tradeoffs. It affects different groups in different ways, redistributing costs and benefits across borrowers, savers, workers, and firms. The effectiveness of policy depends on timing, scale, and the structure of the broader economic system.

Financialization

Financialization refers to the growing influence of financial markets, institutions, and motives in shaping economic activity. It reflects a shift in how value is created, allocated, and measured within the economy. Rather than focusing primarily on production and long-term investment, economic activity becomes more oriented toward financial returns, asset values, and capital markets.

This shift affects how firms operate, how capital is allocated, and how income is distributed. Financial markets provide liquidity and support investment and growth. At the same time, greater reliance on financial mechanisms can change incentives, emphasizing short-term returns over long-term capacity.

Growth of the Financial Sector

The financial sector has expanded significantly relative to the broader economy. In the United States, finance, insurance, and real estate have grown from less than 10 percent of GDP in the mid-20th century to approximately 20 percent in recent decades.[17-01] This growth reflects increased complexity in financial markets, expansion of credit, and the development of new financial instruments.

Financial sector profits have also increased as a share of total corporate profits. At times, the financial sector has accounted for more than 25 percent of total corporate profits, despite employing a much smaller share of the workforce.[17-02] This divergence highlights the concentration of income within financial activities.

The expansion of finance has supported investment and economic growth, but it has also increased the influence of financial incentives on decision-making across industries.

Shift in Corporate Behavior

Financialization has changed how corporations define performance. Traditional measures focused on production, employment, and long-term growth. Increasingly, performance is measured through financial metrics such as earnings per share, return on equity, and stock price.

This shift influences corporate decision-making. Firms may prioritize financial outcomes, including cost reduction, asset optimization, and capital distribution, over long-term investment. Decisions about hiring, wages, and research and development are often evaluated in terms of their impact on financial metrics.

Shareholder value has become a central organizing principle. The objective of maximizing shareholder returns shapes executive incentives, capital allocation, and strategic decisions. While this can improve efficiency, it can also narrow the focus of firms toward financial outcomes.

Share Buybacks and Capital Allocation

Share repurchases are one of the most visible manifestations of financialization. Firms use profits to repurchase their own shares, reducing the number of shares outstanding and increasing earnings per share.

Share buybacks have grown substantially. U.S. corporations have spent trillions of dollars on repurchases over the past two decades, with annual buybacks exceeding $800 billion in recent years.[17-03] These transactions return capital to shareholders but do not directly increase productive capacity.

The use of buybacks affects capital allocation. Funds used for repurchases are not invested in expansion, research, or workforce development. This can influence long-term growth and the distribution of income.

Supporters argue that buybacks return excess capital to investors, allowing it to be redeployed more efficiently. Critics argue that they prioritize short-term financial gains over long-term investment.

Debt Expansion and Leverage

Financialization has been accompanied by increased use of debt. Low interest rates and developed credit markets have made borrowing more accessible, allowing firms to finance operations, acquisitions, and financial transactions.

U.S. nonfinancial corporate debt has grown significantly, exceeding $13 trillion in recent years.[17-04] This increase reflects both investment activity and financial strategies such as leveraged buyouts and share repurchases.

Leverage can enhance returns when conditions are favorable, but it also increases risk. Firms with high debt levels are more sensitive to changes in interest rates and economic conditions. During downturns, debt obligations can constrain operations and lead to restructuring or bankruptcy.

The use of leverage therefore affects both stability and control. It can amplify gains in expansion but magnify losses in contraction.

Asset Price Dependence

Financialization has increased the importance of asset prices in economic outcomes. Equity markets, real estate, and other financial assets influence wealth, consumption, and investment.

Household wealth is increasingly tied to financial markets. Changes in asset prices affect spending behavior, retirement security, and economic confidence. In periods of rising asset values, consumption may increase. When asset prices decline, spending may contract.

This dynamic creates feedback loops. Financial markets influence economic activity, and economic conditions influence financial markets. Volatility in asset prices can therefore have broader economic effects.

Income Distribution and Financial Returns

Financialization affects how income is distributed. Returns to capital, including dividends, interest, and capital gains, have grown relative to labor income. This shift reflects both market dynamics and institutional changes.

Higher-income households hold a larger share of financial assets. As financial returns increase, income becomes more concentrated among those with significant capital holdings. This contributes to differences in wealth and income distribution.

At the same time, wages have grown more slowly in many sectors relative to productivity. This divergence reflects changes in bargaining power, concentration, and the role of capital in production. These trends do not operate uniformly across all sectors, but they illustrate how financial structures influence distributional outcomes.

Financial Innovation and Complexity

Financialization has been supported by innovation in financial instruments and markets. Derivatives, securitization, and structured products have expanded the range of available financial tools. These innovations can improve risk management and liquidity, allowing firms and investors to hedge risk, access capital, and manage exposure to different economic conditions. However, they also increase complexity.

Complex financial instruments can obscure risk and make markets more difficult to monitor. During periods of stress, these complexities can amplify instability, as seen during the 2007–2008 financial crisis. The growth of financial complexity increases the importance of transparency, regulation, and risk management.

Private Equity and Financial Ownership

Private equity has become a significant force in the economy. Firms acquire companies using a combination of equity and debt, often restructuring operations to improve financial performance.

Private equity ownership has expanded across industries, including healthcare, retail, and manufacturing. Global private equity assets under management exceed $10 trillion, reflecting the scale of financial ownership.[17-05] These firms often operate with defined investment horizons, seeking to increase value and exit investments within a specified period. These incentives can drive efficiency but can also prioritize financial returns over long-term stability.

The use of leverage in private equity transactions can further influence outcomes. Debt-financed acquisitions can increase financial risk, particularly if revenue growth falls short of expectations.

Implications for Investment and Production

Financialization affects how capital is allocated between financial and productive uses. Capital can be directed toward financial assets, acquisitions, or shareholder returns rather than new production or capacity. This shift can influence long-term growth. Investment in infrastructure, research, and workforce development may be affected if financial returns are prioritized over productive investment.

At the same time, financial markets provide important functions, allocating capital, supporting innovation, and enabling risk-sharing. The challenge is balancing these functions with the need for long-term investment. The relationship between finance and production is therefore central to economic performance.

Implications for Stability

Financialization can increase both efficiency and fragility. Liquid markets and access to credit support economic activity, but high leverage and interconnected financial systems can amplify shocks.

Periods of financial stress can spread rapidly across markets and sectors. Changes in credit conditions, asset prices, or confidence can affect investment, employment, and consumption.

Regulation and oversight aim to manage these risks. Capital requirements, transparency rules, and monitoring systems are designed to reduce systemic vulnerability.

However, financial innovation can outpace regulatory frameworks, requiring continual adaptation.

Implications for the System

Financialization reshapes the relationship between capital, labor, and production. It influences how decisions are made, how resources are allocated, and how value is distributed. When financial incentives dominate, economic activity may prioritize returns on capital over long-term capacity. When balanced with productive investment, financial systems can support growth and innovation.

The structure of financial systems affects the broader economy. It determines how capital flows, how risk is distributed, and how resilient the system is to disruption.

Understanding financialization is necessary to understand modern economic outcomes. It reflects the increasing role of financial structures in shaping incentives, decisions, and results. These financial structures determine how capital is allocated, which industries expand, how firms are organized, and how risk is distributed. The effects are most visible in work, in how jobs are created, organized, and how income is generated and sustained.

To understand work, it is therefore necessary to understand how financial systems shape economic structure.

SECTION IV — Work and Economic Structure

The Role of Work in Human Life

Work is more than income. It is how individuals sustain themselves, maintain independence, and participate in society. It supports liberty by enabling self-reliance, and it reinforces purpose and connection through contribution. In modern economies, most households depend on earned income as their primary source of support, linking economic systems directly to daily life.[18-01]

Independence is Liberty

Independence depends on the ability to provide for oneself. Income earned through work allows individuals to make choices about housing, food, healthcare, and family life. Without that independence, choices narrow and reliance on others or on public support increases. In this way, work underpins liberty in everyday life, as economic dependence can limit freedom even when legal rights remain intact.

Work is also the primary means of survival. For most individuals, earnings from labor represent the majority of household income, and disruptions in employment have immediate consequences. When work is stable, individuals can plan, save, and invest in the future. When work is unstable or unavailable, housing becomes uncertain, access to healthcare declines, and financial stress increases. These pressures often extend beyond the individual to families and dependents, affecting long-term stability.

Beyond survival, work provides purpose and structure. It establishes routine, creates goals, and connects effort to outcome. The ability to contribute, to produce something of value, and to be recognized for that contribution reinforces personal dignity. When that connection weakens, the effects are not only economic. Research shows that unemployment is associated with increased rates of depression, substance abuse, and social isolation, reflecting the broader impact of job loss on well-being.[18-02]

Work also serves as a primary form of participation in society. Through work, individuals contribute to goods, services, and systems that others rely on. This participation creates interdependence, linking individuals to broader economic and social structures. Employment is often the primary point of contact with institutions such as healthcare systems, retirement systems, and financial services. When participation through work declines, engagement with these systems often declines as well.

The nature of work has changed over time. In agrarian economies, most work was tied to land, family, and direct production of food. Industrialization shifted work into factories and centralized production, creating wage labor and large-scale employment. The modern service economy has further changed how work is organized, emphasizing information, technology, and services rather than physical production. Today, service industries account for the majority of employment in the United States, representing more than 80 percent of total employment.[18-03]

These changes have increased productivity and expanded opportunity, but they have also introduced new forms of instability. The move from long-term employment toward more flexible or fragmented work arrangements changes how risk is distributed. Alternative work arrangements, including contract, temporary, and gig work, have expanded, as mentioned earlier, with estimates indicating that roughly 10 to 15 percent of workers participate in these arrangements as a primary or supplemental source of income.[18-04]

In earlier systems, families or firms often absorbed fluctuations. In modern arrangements, individuals more often bear that risk directly through variable income, limited benefits, and less predictable work.

The role of work remains constant even as its structure evolves. It provides income, supports independence, reinforces dignity, and connects individuals to society. When access to stable and meaningful work is disrupted, the effects extend beyond economics. Long-term unemployment is associated with higher rates of poverty, reduced life expectancy, and increased social instability, reflecting the broader consequences of economic disruption.[18-05]

Understanding that role is necessary to understand how economic systems affect everyday life and how changes in those systems reshape opportunity, risk, and participation.

Job Structure and Employment Types

Work is organized through a range of employment structures that determine how income is earned, how risk is distributed, and how individuals participate in the economy. These structures include full-time employment, part-time work, contract labor, temporary work, and self-employment. Each form differs in stability, compensation, benefits, and exposure to economic fluctuations.

The structure of employment is not fixed. It evolves in response to technology, market conditions, and policy. As these factors change, so do the types of jobs available, the terms of employment, and the distribution of risk between firms and workers.

Traditional Employment

Full-time employment has historically been the dominant form of work in industrial economies. It is typically characterized by a stable schedule, regular wages or salary, and access to employer-provided benefits such as health insurance and retirement plans. This model provides predictability for both workers and employers.

Employer-provided benefits are a central feature of traditional employment in the United States. A majority of full-time workers receive health insurance through their employer, linking employment directly to access to healthcare.[18-06] Retirement benefits, including defined contribution plans such as 401(k)s, are also commonly tied to employment.

Stable employment supports long-term planning. Workers can rely on consistent income and benefits, allowing them to make decisions about housing, education, and savings. For employers, stable employment relationships support training, productivity, and retention.

However, traditional employment also involves fixed costs. Employers must commit to wages, benefits, and regulatory requirements. During economic downturns, these obligations can lead to layoffs or hiring freezes as firms adjust to changing conditions.

Part-Time and Temporary Work

Part-time and temporary employment provide flexibility in labor markets. These arrangements allow firms to adjust staffing levels in response to demand and enable workers to participate in the labor force under varying circumstances.

Part-time employment accounts for a significant share of the workforce, with roughly 15 to 20 percent of workers employed on a part-time basis.[18-07] Some workers choose part-time work for flexibility, while others accept it due to limited full-time opportunities.

Temporary employment and staffing arrangements also play a role in labor markets. These positions can provide entry into the workforce or serve as a bridge between jobs. However, they often offer lower wages and fewer benefits than full-time positions.

These forms of employment increase flexibility but may reduce stability. Income can be variable, and access to benefits is often limited. Workers in these arrangements may face greater uncertainty in scheduling and earnings.

Contract and Gig Work

Contract and gig work have expanded with the growth of digital platforms and changes in business organization. In these arrangements, workers are typically classified as independent contractors rather than employees.

Independent contractors generally receive payment per task or project rather than a fixed wage, with responsibility for taxes, benefits, and insurance. This shift moves responsibility from firms to individuals.

Estimates indicate that a significant portion of the workforce participates in alternative work arrangements, including independent contracting and gig work, either as a primary or supplemental source of income.[18-04] These arrangements provide flexibility and autonomy but often lack the protections associated with traditional employment.

The growth of platform-based work has increased access to short-term opportunities. At the same time, it has raised questions about income stability, worker classification, and access to benefits. The classification of workers as employees or independent contractors affects wages, protections, and legal rights.

Self-Employment and Entrepreneurship

Self-employment represents another form of work organization. Individuals operate their own businesses or provide services directly to clients. This model offers autonomy and the potential for higher returns but also involves greater risk.

Self-employed individuals are responsible for generating income, managing expenses, and securing benefits. Income can be variable, and business conditions can change rapidly. In the United States, self-employment accounts for roughly 10 percent of the workforce, reflecting a consistent but limited share of total employment.[18-08]

Entrepreneurship can drive innovation and economic growth. New firms introduce products, services, and business models that expand markets and create employment. However, new business formation also carries a high rate of failure, and income is often uncertain in the early stages.

The balance between opportunity and risk defines self-employment. It provides a pathway to independence but requires individuals to absorb economic uncertainty directly.

Job Stability and Risk Distribution

Employment structures determine how economic risk is distributed between firms and workers. In traditional employment, firms absorb a larger share of risk by providing stable wages and benefits. In more flexible arrangements, risk shifts toward workers.

Job stability has declined in some sectors. Measures of job tenure indicate that workers are less likely to remain with a single employer for extended periods compared to earlier decades.[18-09] Increased job mobility reflects both opportunity and instability.

Economic fluctuations affect employment differently depending on structure. Workers in temporary, part-time, or contract roles are often more exposed to changes in demand. These positions may be reduced more quickly during downturns.

The distribution of risk affects income stability, access to benefits, and long-term security. It also influences how workers respond to economic change, including their willingness to invest in skills or change jobs.

Benefits and Employment

Access to benefits is closely tied to employment structure. Full-time employees are more likely to receive employer-provided health insurance, retirement plans, and paid leave. In contrast, part-time, temporary, and contract workers often have limited access to these benefits.

Approximately half of private-sector workers participate in employer-sponsored retirement plans, reflecting variation in access across employment types.[18-10] Health insurance coverage also varies, with full-time employees significantly more likely to receive employer-sponsored coverage than part-time or contract workers.

These differences affect financial security and long-term planning. Workers without access to benefits must obtain them independently or go without, increasing exposure to financial risk.

The link between employment and benefits creates structural differences in economic security. Changes in employment patterns therefore have direct implications for healthcare access, retirement savings, and income stability.

Technology and Job Structure

Technological change is reshaping job structure. Automation, artificial intelligence, and digital platforms are altering how work is performed and how labor is organized. These changes affect both the quantity and type of jobs available.

Automation can replace routine tasks, reducing demand for certain types of labor while increasing demand for others.

Studies estimate that a significant share of current tasks could be automated using existing technologies, although the pace and extent of adoption vary.[18-11]

Digital platforms enable new forms of work organization, including remote work and on-demand labor. These systems can increase efficiency and expand access to opportunities but may also contribute to fragmentation of work.

Technology therefore influences both productivity and employment structure. It changes how firms organize labor and how workers engage with the economy.

Implications for Economic Outcomes

Job structure and employment types shape how income is earned and how risk is distributed, influencing stability, access to benefits, and opportunities for advancement. Differences in employment structure contribute to differences in economic outcomes across individuals and households.

Flexible work arrangements can increase access to employment and allow for adaptation to changing conditions. However, they can also reduce predictability and shift risk to workers. Traditional employment provides stability but may limit flexibility.

The balance between these structures affects economic resilience. Systems that provide both flexibility and security can support participation and stability. Systems that concentrate risk on individuals may increase vulnerability.

Understanding job structure is necessary to understand how economic systems operate at the individual level. It connects broader economic forces to daily experience, shaping how people earn income, manage risk, and participate in society.

The Changing Nature of Work

Work is changing in ways that affect how income is earned, how risk is distributed, and how economic stability is maintained. Automation, digital platforms, and changes in business organization are altering the relationship between workers and employers. These developments are part of a broader transition tied to the expansion of artificial intelligence and its growing role in economic activity.

Nature of Automation

Automation has long replaced specific tasks, but recent advances extend beyond manual labor into cognitive work. Systems that can process language, analyze data, and generate content are now performing functions previously limited to human workers. Studies estimate that up to 60 percent of current occupations have at least 30 percent of tasks that could be automated with existing technology, indicating a broad potential impact on labor demand.[18-11] As a result, productivity gains do not necessarily translate into proportional employment gains, particularly where automation substitutes for labor rather than complements it.

At the same time, the organization of work has shifted away from long-term employment relationships toward more flexible and fragmented arrangements. The traditional model, in which individuals worked for a single employer over extended periods with stable wages and employer-provided benefits, has declined in many sectors. In its place, a range of alternative arrangements has expanded, including contract work, freelance services, and platform-mediated labor.

Estimates indicate that a substantial share of the workforce now participates in some form of independent or nontraditional work. Roughly 15 to 20 percent of workers rely on independent or contract work as a primary source of income, while a larger share, often 30 to 40 percent, engages in such work at least part time or as supplemental income.[18-04] These figures reflect a structural shift rather than a temporary trend and indicate that nontraditional work arrangements are becoming a persistent feature of the labor market.

The gig economy illustrates this change. Digital platforms match labor to demand in real time, assigning work on a task-by-task basis. This model reduces coordination costs for firms and increases flexibility for workers, but it also changes how risk is distributed. Income becomes less predictable, hours fluctuate, and workers are responsible for managing taxes, insurance, and retirement savings. The absence of employer-provided benefits transfers responsibilities that were once shared into individual obligations.

Job tenure has also declined. Workers are less likely to remain with a single employer for extended periods, particularly in private-sector roles. Median job tenure in the United States is approximately four years overall and lower in many industries, especially among younger workers.[18-09] Shorter tenure reflects both voluntary mobility and structural change, as firms adjust staffing levels more frequently and rely more heavily on contingent labor.

Remote work has further altered the structure of employment. As of recent estimates, approximately 22 to 23 percent of U.S. workers perform their jobs remotely at least part of the time, with hybrid arrangements becoming common in many sectors.[18-12] Remote work expands access to labor markets and allows firms to source talent across geographic boundaries. It also increases competition, as workers may compete not only locally but nationally or globally for the same roles.

These shifts affect how benefits are provided. Under traditional employment, firms often provided health insurance, retirement plans, and other forms of support. As work becomes more fragmented, these benefits are increasingly self-funded. Individuals must secure health coverage, manage retirement contributions, and absorb periods of unemployment without institutional support. This change increases financial risk, particularly for workers with unstable income.

The cumulative effect is a transition from employment-based security to income-based uncertainty. Work is increasingly organized around discrete tasks and short-term relationships rather than long-term roles. While this model can increase flexibility and efficiency, it also reduces predictability and shifts responsibility for risk management to individuals.

Artificial intelligence is likely to accelerate these trends. As more tasks become automated, the boundary between human and machine labor will continue to shift. Some jobs will be redefined, others will be eliminated, and new roles will emerge. Estimates suggest that generative AI alone could affect tasks representing a significant share of current work activities, particularly in knowledge-based occupations.[18-13] The pace of this change may exceed the ability of existing institutions to adapt, particularly where education, training, and labor policies are not aligned with evolving demands.

How work is organized therefore matters not only for economic output, but for stability, mobility, and social conditions. When work becomes more fragmented and less predictable, the effects extend beyond individual workers to households, communities, and the broader economy. Understanding how these changes interact with technological advancement is necessary to assess how work, jobs, and economic security are likely to evolve.

Jobs, Wages, and Economic Mobility

Work has long been the primary path through which individuals improve their economic position. Wages determine not only immediate income but also the ability to build savings, invest in education, secure housing, and provide stability for families. In the United States, labor income remains the primary source of earnings for most households, linking employment directly to economic mobility.18-01 When wages grow in line with productivity and living costs, work supports upward mobility. When they do not, mobility slows and, for many, stops.

Economic mobility depends on more than employment alone. The type of work available, the level of compensation, and the stability of that work influence whether individuals can advance or remain financially constrained. Jobs that lack sufficient income, predictable hours, or opportunities for advancement limit mobility even when employment is continuous.

Productivity and Wage Growth

Over the past several decades, a gap has emerged between productivity growth and wage growth. Since the late 1970s, output per worker has increased substantially, while median wages have grown more slowly in real terms. Estimates indicate that productivity has increased by more than 60 percent since the late 1970s, while median hourly compensation has risen by a much smaller margin after adjusting for inflation.[18-14]

This divergence indicates that gains in economic output have not translated evenly into higher earnings for the typical worker. While higher-income households have seen stronger growth, wage gains for middle- and lower-income workers have been more limited. As a result, economic growth has not produced proportional increases in purchasing power across the population.

Inflation and Real Income

Inflation further complicates wage growth. Nominal wages may increase, but when those increases fail to exceed rising costs for housing, healthcare, education, and essential goods, real purchasing power remains unchanged. Periods of higher inflation can reduce real income even when wages rise, limiting the ability of households to build savings or improve their financial position.[18-04]

These effects are not evenly distributed. Households with limited income flexibility are more exposed to rising costs, particularly for essential goods. As a result, inflation can reduce effective income and constrain upward mobility even in periods of nominal wage growth.

Wealth and Capital Accumulation

Wealth distribution reflects these patterns over time. As of recent estimates, and as said earlier, the top 10 percent of households hold roughly two-thirds of total household wealth in the United States, while the bottom 50 percent hold only a small share, often in the range of 2 to 3 percent.[18-15]

Because wealth generates returns through investment, differences in asset ownership compound over time. Individuals who rely primarily on wages must use current income to cover living expenses, leaving limited capacity to accumulate assets. Those with access to capital benefit from returns that are not directly tied to labor, allowing wealth to grow independently of work.

This dynamic affects economic mobility. Differences in asset ownership influence access to education, housing, and investment opportunities, shaping long-term financial outcomes.

Employment Structure and Stability

The structure of employment also affects mobility. Stable, full-time positions with benefits have become less common in some sectors, replaced by contract, part-time, or platform-based work. These arrangements can provide flexibility but often shift risk to workers, including income volatility, limited benefits, and reduced access to retirement systems.[18-04]

When work becomes less predictable, the ability to plan, save, and invest declines. Irregular income and limited benefits increase financial uncertainty, making it more difficult to build long-term stability.

Employment structure therefore influences not only income levels but also the distribution of risk within the economy.

Geographic and Sector Differences

Economic mobility varies across regions and industries. Wage levels, job availability, and cost of living differ significantly across geographic areas. A wage that provides stability in one region may be insufficient in another, particularly where housing and essential costs are higher.

Industries also differ in their capacity to support advancement. High-skill and capital-intensive sectors tend to offer stronger wage growth and career progression. Lower-wage sectors often provide limited opportunities for advancement, even with continuous employment.

These differences affect access to opportunity and influence long-term economic outcomes.

Education and Opportunity

Education and training remain important determinants of income and mobility. Higher levels of education are generally associated with higher earnings and lower unemployment. However, access to education varies, and the cost of education has increased significantly.

Student loan balances in the United States exceed $1.7 trillion, reflecting the scale of investment required for higher education.[18-16] While education can improve earnings, mobility is not guaranteed. In some cases, individuals incur substantial debt without corresponding income gains.

The alignment between education and labor market demand also affects outcomes. When skills do not match available jobs, the benefits of education are reduced.

Implications for Economic Mobility

Work remains the primary path to economic mobility for most individuals, but that path has narrowed in important ways. When wage growth lags behind productivity, when inflation erodes purchasing power, and when employment becomes less stable, upward movement becomes more difficult.

Mobility depends not only on individual effort but on the structure of the economy. Access to stable employment, sufficient wages, and opportunities for advancement all influence whether individuals can improve their economic position.

Understanding how jobs and wages interact with these broader forces is necessary to understand how economic outcomes are determined and how opportunity is created or constrained.

Education and Workforce Alignment

Education and workforce alignment determines whether a labor force can meet current demand, adapt to change, and translate work into stable income and upward mobility.

Skills Mismatch and Labor Demand

Economic change depends on the ability of workers to adapt, but education and training systems do not always keep pace with shifting labor demands. When the skills required for available jobs differ from the skills workers possess, the result is a mismatch that limits mobility, slows growth, and leaves both employers and workers at a disadvantage.

This mismatch appears across sectors. In recent surveys, more than 75 percent of employers report difficulty filling roles, particularly those requiring technical, digital, and specialized skills.[19-05] At the same time, millions of workers remain underemployed or outside the labor force. Job openings in the United States have exceeded unemployed workers in multiple periods since 2018, indicating not only a shortage of labor, but a mismatch of skills.[19-05]

The gap is not limited to advanced degrees. Middle-skill jobs, those requiring more than a high school diploma but less than a four-year degree, account for roughly half of all positions in the economy, yet the training pipeline for these roles remains underdeveloped.[19-15] Skilled trades, technical certifications, and applied training programs often lack visibility, funding, or structured pathways. When training is misaligned with labor market demand, positions remain unfilled even as unemployment persists elsewhere.

Education Costs and Economic Risk

The cost of education compounds this problem. Higher education is often treated as the primary path to economic mobility, yet it carries significant financial risk. Outstanding student loan debt in the United States exceeds $1.7 trillion, with more than 40 million borrowers.[19-08,19-10] Average debt for bachelor's degree recipients is approximately $30,000, with many borrowers carrying substantially higher balances.[19-09]

This debt affects economic behavior. Studies indicate that student debt delays home ownership, reduces small business formation, and limits geographic mobility.[19-11] For individuals whose degrees do not lead to sufficient income gains, repayment obligations can offset much of the economic benefit of education. Default and delinquency rates remain elevated among borrowers who did not complete a degree or entered lower-paying fields.[19-11]

Returns to education vary widely by field of study and institution. While some degrees generate strong income gains, others produce limited or uncertain returns. The result is an uneven system in which individuals assume financial risk without clear alignment between education and labor market demand.

Lifelong Learning and Technological Change

Technological change is increasing the rate at which skills become obsolete. Traditional education models are front-loaded, concentrating learning in early adulthood, while the modern economy requires continuous adaptation. New technologies, including artificial intelligence and automation, can alter job requirements within a few years.

Estimates suggest that a significant share of the workforce, often cited in the range of 30 to 40 percent, will require reskilling or upskilling within the next decade due to automation and digital transformation.[19-06] [19-12] Digital skills alone are now required in the majority of occupations, including roles that previously did not require advanced technical knowledge.[19-06]

Despite this need, participation in adult training remains limited. Fewer than half of working-age adults engage in formal education or training in a given year, and access is uneven.[19-20] Time constraints, cost, and lack of employer support reduce participation, particularly among lower-income workers who face the greatest risk of displacement.

Training Systems and Incentive Structures

Job training programs illustrate the gap between need and execution. Public and private training initiatives exist, but they often lack coordination with employer demand or fail to scale effectively. Funding is fragmented across federal, state, and local programs, each with different requirements and objectives.

Some programs focus on short-term placement rather than building transferable skills. Others require time and financial commitments that are not feasible for working adults. Completion rates for many workforce training programs remain low, and outcomes vary widely by program and region.[19-13]

Employer incentives also shape outcomes. Many firms underinvest in training due to concerns about employee turnover. If workers can leave after gaining new skills, the return on training investment is uncertain. This creates a collective action problem, where firms benefit from a skilled workforce but hesitate to bear the cost of developing it.[19-21]

As a result, workers often bear the responsibility for financing and managing their own skill development, even when the benefits extend beyond the individual to employers and the broader economy.

System Lag and Structural Constraints

The pace of change intensifies the challenge. Advances in automation and digital systems are reshaping industries faster than education systems can adjust curricula, accreditation standards, and delivery methods. Program approval processes, institutional incentives, and regulatory requirements slow adaptation.

By the time training programs are updated, the underlying skills demand may have shifted again. This lag creates a structural disadvantage, particularly for workers in roles vulnerable to technological displacement, including administrative support, routine manufacturing, and certain service occupations.[19-17]

Regional differences further complicate alignment. Labor demand varies across locations, but training systems are often not responsive to local economic conditions. Workers may not have access to training programs that match opportunities in their region, and relocation is limited by cost and personal constraints.

Employment Transitions and Economic Outcomes

The consequences extend beyond employment. When individuals cannot transition effectively between roles, periods of unemployment lengthen, income becomes unstable, and upward mobility slows. Long-term unemployment reduces future earnings potential, with wage scarring effects that can persist for years.[19-19]

Labor force participation declines when displaced workers do not find suitable opportunities. This reduces overall economic output and increases reliance on public support systems. Over time, these effects accumulate, contributing to broader disparities in opportunity and economic security.

Income volatility also increases when workers move between unstable or mismatched roles. Without clear pathways for advancement, employment becomes less effective as a mechanism for improving economic position.

Alignment, Flexibility, and Continuous Development

Addressing this gap requires more than expanding access to traditional education. It requires alignment between training pathways and labor demand, greater flexibility in how skills are acquired and recognized, and systems that support continuous learning throughout working life.

This includes clearer signaling of labor market needs, stronger connections between employers and training providers, and alternative credentialing systems that recognize skills gained outside traditional degree programs. Apprenticeships, modular credentials, and employer-partnered training models can improve alignment when scaled effectively.

Incentives must also be aligned across individuals, employers, and institutions. When training investments produce shared benefits, costs and risks must also be shared. Without that alignment, workers will continue to face barriers to skill development, and employers will continue to face skill shortages.

Without structural alignment between education and labor demand, the ability of workers to adapt will continue to lag behind the pace of economic change, narrowing the path to stability, mobility, and long-term economic security.

Labor Market Flexibility and Risk Transfer

Labor market flexibility determines how easily workers and firms adjust to change, but the structure of that flexibility also determines who bears economic risk when conditions shift.

Forms of Labor Market Flexibility

Labor markets adjust through multiple mechanisms, including hiring, layoffs, wages, hours, and job structure. Firms seek flexibility to respond to demand, control costs, and manage uncertainty. Workers seek stability, predictable income, and access to benefits. These objectives are often in tension.

Over time, the U.S. labor market has become more flexible in how work is structured. Nontraditional work arrangements, including part-time, temporary, contract, and gig work, have expanded. Estimates suggest that approximately 10 to 15 percent of workers participate in alternative work arrangements as a primary or secondary source of income, with higher participation in certain sectors.[20-01]

Flexible work arrangements can increase labor market participation and provide income opportunities, particularly for individuals seeking supplemental earnings or nonstandard schedules. At the same time, these arrangements often differ from traditional employment in stability, benefits, and income predictability.

Risk Allocation Between Employers and Workers

Flexibility changes how risk is distributed. In traditional employment, firms assume a larger share of risk through stable wages, benefits, and long-term employment relationships. In more flexible arrangements, a greater share of risk shifts to workers.

This shift is evident in multiple dimensions. Variable scheduling transfers demand risk to employees, whose hours and income may fluctuate week to week. Independent contractors and gig workers assume responsibility for equipment, insurance, and unpaid time. Benefits such as health insurance, retirement contributions, and paid leave are often reduced or absent outside standard employment relationships.

Income volatility reflects this shift. A substantial share of workers experience significant month-to-month income variation, with lower-income households facing the greatest instability.20-02 Without mechanisms to smooth income, workers must absorb short-term fluctuations, increasing financial vulnerability.

Benefits, Security, and Coverage Gaps

Employment-based benefits are a central component of economic security in the United States. Health insurance, retirement savings, and paid leave are often tied to full-time employment. As work arrangements become more flexible, access to these benefits becomes less consistent.

Approximately half of private-sector workers participate in employer-sponsored retirement plans, and access is significantly lower among part-time and lower-wage workers.20-03 Health insurance coverage also varies by employment status, with nontraditional workers more likely to rely on individual markets or remain uninsured.[20-04]

The structure of benefits creates gaps when workers move between jobs or work outside traditional employment. Benefits are not always portable, and eligibility requirements can exclude workers with variable hours or multiple employers. As a result, flexibility in employment can reduce continuity in coverage, even when individuals remain active in the labor force.

Wages, Bargaining, and Market Power

Labor market flexibility also interacts with wage determination. In markets with strong competition for labor, flexibility can increase opportunities and wages. In markets with limited competition, flexibility can weaken worker bargaining power.

Measures of labor market concentration indicate that many local labor markets are dominated by a small number of employers, reducing competition for workers.20-05 In these settings, workers have fewer alternatives, limiting their ability to negotiate wages and working conditions.

Union membership has declined from approximately 20 percent of the workforce in the early 1980s to about 10 percent today, reducing collective bargaining power in many sectors.[20-06] At the same time, the use of noncompete agreements and other contractual restrictions can limit worker mobility, further affecting wage growth.[20-07]

When bargaining power is uneven, the benefits of flexibility may accrue more to firms than to workers, particularly in lower-wage or highly concentrated markets.

Employment Stability and Adjustment

Flexibility affects how quickly labor markets adjust to economic changes. In periods of expansion, flexible arrangements can facilitate hiring and allow firms to scale operations. In downturns, they can accelerate job losses or reductions in hours.

The United States generally exhibits higher rates of job turnover than many other advanced economies. Workers change jobs more frequently, and firms adjust employment levels more rapidly.[20-08] This dynamism can support innovation and reallocation of resources, but it can also increase employment instability.

Short job tenure and frequent transitions can disrupt income, benefits, and career progression. While some workers benefit from mobility, others experience repeated periods of instability without sustained wage growth.

Technology, Scheduling, and Control

Technology has increased the ability of firms to manage labor in real time. Digital platforms, scheduling software, and data analytics enable more precise matching of labor supply to demand. This can improve efficiency, but it can also shift uncertainty onto workers.

Algorithmic scheduling systems can adjust hours with little notice, making income and work schedules less predictable. Platform-based work often relies on dynamic pricing and task allocation, where earnings depend on demand conditions outside the worker's control.

These systems can expand access to work, but they also reduce predictability. For workers without financial buffers, even small fluctuations in hours or pay can have significant effects on economic stability.

Risk, Mobility, and Economic Outcomes

The distribution of risk affects economic outcomes over time. When risk is concentrated on workers, income volatility increases, savings become more difficult, and exposure to financial shocks grows.

Research indicates that a large share of households would have difficulty covering an unexpected expense without borrowing or selling assets, reflecting limited financial buffers.20-09 Income instability can reduce consumption, delay investment in education or training, and increase reliance on credit.

Mobility is also affected. Workers may be less likely to change jobs, relocate, or pursue new opportunities when doing so involves losing benefits or taking on additional risk. This can reduce the efficiency of labor market matching and limit long-term income growth.

Balancing Flexibility and Security

Labor market flexibility provides important advantages, including adaptability, innovation, and expanded participation. The challenge is not flexibility itself, but how its costs and benefits are distributed.

Systems that balance flexibility with security can support both adjustment and stability. This includes mechanisms that smooth income, expand access to benefits, and maintain mobility across jobs and work arrangements.

Approaches may include portable benefits, broader access to retirement and health coverage, and policies that reduce barriers to mobility. The objective is not to eliminate flexibility, but to ensure that the risks associated with it do not fall disproportionately on those least able to absorb them.

Without that balance, labor market flexibility can shift from a source of economic dynamism to a source of instability, increasing risk for workers while limiting the long-term benefits of a changing economy.

Workforce Participation

Workforce participation determines how much of a population is engaged in economic activity, shaping labor supply, economic output, and the distribution of income across society.

Participation Rates and Labor Supply

The labor force participation rate measures the share of the working-age population that is either employed or actively seeking work. Changes in participation affect the size of the labor force and the economy's capacity to produce goods and services.

In the United States, labor force participation rose steadily through the latter half of the twentieth century, driven in part by increased participation among women. Since around 2000, overall participation has declined, influenced by demographic changes, including the aging of the population, as well as shifts in labor demand.[20-10]

Prime-age participation, typically defined as individuals ages 25 to 54, provides a clearer measure of labor market engagement. While participation among this group has recovered in recent years, it remains below peak levels observed in prior decades.[20-10]

Participation varies significantly by age, education, and region, reflecting differences in opportunities, incentives, and barriers to employment.

Demographics and Structural Change

Demographic trends play a central role in workforce participation. As the population ages, a larger share of individuals move into retirement, reducing overall participation rates. The proportion of the U.S. population aged 65 and older has increased steadily and is projected to continue rising, placing downward pressure on labor force growth.[20-11]

At the same time, younger cohorts face different labor market conditions than previous generations. Delayed entry into the workforce due to extended education, as well as changes in job availability, can affect early career participation and long-term earnings trajectories.

Immigration also influences labor supply. Immigrants account for a meaningful share of labor force growth, particularly in certain industries and regions. Changes in immigration policy can therefore affect participation rates and the availability of labor in key sectors.[20-12]

These demographic factors interact with economic conditions, shaping both the supply of workers and the types of jobs available.

Barriers to Participation

Workforce participation is influenced not only by the availability of jobs, but also by barriers that limit the ability or willingness of individuals to work.

Health is a significant factor. Chronic conditions, disability, and access to healthcare can affect an individual's capacity to participate in the labor force. Increases in disability claims and health-related work limitations have been associated with lower participation in some populations.[20-13]

Caregiving responsibilities also affect participation. Access to affordable childcare influences labor force participation, particularly among parents of young children.

When childcare costs are high relative to wages, participation declines.[20-14]

Other barriers include transportation, education and skill mismatches, and geographic constraints. In some regions, job opportunities may be limited, while in others, housing costs may prevent workers from relocating to areas with stronger demand.

Incentives within public programs can also affect participation. Eligibility thresholds for benefits such as disability insurance, unemployment insurance, and means-tested programs can create situations where additional earnings result in reduced benefits, affecting work decisions at the margin.

Participation and Wage Dynamics

Participation rates interact with wages through labor supply. When participation is high, the supply of available workers increases, which can moderate wage growth. When participation is low, labor shortages can place upward pressure on wages.

However, the relationship is not uniform across sectors or regions. In some areas, low participation reflects structural barriers rather than voluntary withdrawal from the labor force. In these cases, wages may not adjust sufficiently to attract workers if barriers remain in place.

Wage growth also influences participation decisions. Higher wages can draw individuals into the labor force, particularly among groups with historically lower participation rates. Conversely, stagnant wages can reduce incentives to work, especially when combined with other costs such as childcare, transportation, or healthcare.

Long-Term Nonparticipation and Detachment

A portion of the population remains outside the labor force for extended periods. Long-term nonparticipation can lead to skill erosion, reduced employability, and lower lifetime earnings.

Prime-age male participation has declined over several decades, reflecting a combination of factors including structural changes in the economy, reduced demand for certain types of labor, and other social and economic influences.[20-15]

Extended absence from the labor force can make reentry more difficult. Employers may view gaps in employment as a signal of reduced skills or reliability, even when the underlying causes are unrelated to job performance.

Detachment from the labor force also has broader economic effects. Lower participation reduces overall output and can increase reliance on public support systems. Over time, these effects contribute to disparities in income and opportunity.

Participation, Productivity, and Growth

Workforce participation contributes directly to economic growth by increasing the number of people engaged in production. It also interacts with productivity, as the composition of the labor force affects the types of work performed and the efficiency with which it is carried out.

Higher participation can support economic growth, particularly when it involves individuals with skills that match labor market demand. However, participation alone is not sufficient. The quality of employment, including wages, stability, and opportunities for advancement, also determines economic outcomes.

When participation increases in low-wage or unstable roles, the effect on income and mobility may be limited. Conversely, increasing participation in higher-productivity sectors can contribute more significantly to economic growth and individual advancement.

Incentives, Access, and Engagement

Workforce participation reflects the interaction of incentives, access, and opportunity. Individuals are more likely to participate when work provides sufficient income, stability, and prospects for advancement.

Policies that affect wages, benefits, and working conditions influence participation decisions. Access to education, training, childcare, and healthcare also shapes the ability to work. Geographic and technological factors determine where and how work is available.

Engagement in the labor force depends not only on the availability of jobs, but on whether those jobs provide a viable path to economic security. When work lacks stability or opportunity for advancement, participation may decline, particularly among those with alternative sources of support.

Participation and Economic Outcomes

The level and composition of workforce participation affect the distribution of income and the overall performance of the economy. Higher participation can increase total output, broaden the tax base, and reduce reliance on public assistance.

At the same time, disparities in participation contribute to disparities in income and opportunity. Groups with lower participation rates often experience lower earnings, reduced wealth accumulation, and greater economic vulnerability.

Improving participation requires addressing both supply and demand factors. This includes reducing barriers to work, aligning skills with labor market needs, and ensuring that employment provides sufficient returns to justify participation.

Without sustained participation across a broad share of the population, economic growth becomes more limited, and the benefits of that growth become more unevenly distributed.

SECTION V — Technology and Future Systems

Robotics and Physical Automation

Robotics and physical automation extend digital systems into the physical world, allowing software to sense, decide, and act on real objects, environments, and processes, changing how work is performed and how production systems are organized.

Task Structure and Automation Boundaries

Robotics rarely replaces entire jobs. It replaces specific tasks. Most work consists of multiple tasks, some structured and repetitive, others variable and judgment-based. Automation succeeds where tasks are consistent, measurable, and performed in controlled environments. It is more difficult where objects vary, conditions change, or outcomes depend on nuanced physical interaction. The result is not the elimination of work, but the reallocation of tasks between humans and machines.

This distinction defines where automation can be deployed effectively. Tasks that are predictable and repeatable can be automated with high reliability. Tasks that require adaptation, judgment, or complex interaction remain more dependent on human capability. As a result, automation changes the composition of jobs rather than eliminating them entirely.

Industrial Robotics and Production Systems

In manufacturing, robotics has been deployed for decades, particularly in applications such as welding, painting, and assembly where precision and repeatability are critical. Global installations of industrial robots have exceeded 500,000 units annually in recent years, with an operational stock of approximately 4.3 million robots worldwide.[21-01] The density of robots in manufacturing has also increased, reflecting the growing role of automation in production systems.[21-02]

These systems are most effective where workflows are highly structured, parts are standardized, and variability is minimized. Production processes are often designed around the capabilities of automation, using controlled inputs and defined sequences to reduce uncertainty. In these environments, robots can operate with consistent cycle times and predictable outcomes, increasing both efficiency and quality.

As automation expands, it changes how production is organized. Systems become more dependent on capital investment, integration, and maintenance, and less dependent on manual repetition. This shift alters how firms organize work and how they compete across industries.

Logistics Automation and Service Environments

Outside of manufacturing, robotics has expanded rapidly into logistics, warehousing, and service environments. Autonomous mobile robots now move goods, coordinate with inventory systems, and support order fulfillment. Large-scale deployments include more than one million robots operating within a single logistics network.[21-08]

In these environments, robots handle movement and positioning while humans manage oversight, exceptions, and coordination. Work shifts away from physical transport toward system interaction. This can increase throughput and reduce physical strain, but it also changes the skill profile required for many roles.

Service robotics extends into areas such as cleaning, inspection, agriculture, and healthcare support. These environments are less structured than manufacturing, which limits full automation and increases reliance on systems where humans and machines operate together.

Technical Constraints and System Integration

Robotics is often described as an extension of artificial intelligence, but physical automation introduces constraints that do not exist in digital systems. Software must operate within real-world variability, including differences in object shape, weight, position, and environmental conditions. Tasks that appear simple for humans, such as handling mixed or deformable items, remain difficult to automate reliably.

The primary challenge is not the performance of the robot in isolation, but the performance of the full system. Successful deployment depends on integration with fixturing, part presentation, error recovery, maintenance, and coordination with upstream and downstream processes. Systems that perform well in controlled demonstrations may fail in production when variability and wear are introduced.

Effective automation often requires redesigning workflows to match the capabilities of the system. This includes standardizing inputs, reducing variability, and explicitly managing exceptions. Without these adjustments, automation can increase complexity without improving outcomes.

Economics of Automation and System Performance

The economic value of robotics is determined by system performance rather than the presence of automation itself. Outcomes are measured in throughput, quality, uptime, and reliability. A system that operates at a consistent cycle time can stabilize production and reduce variability.

Automation is frequently adopted in response to labor shortages, high turnover, or physically demanding work. In these cases, robots provide consistency and reduce disruption. Improvements in quality and reductions in defects can also generate significant value, particularly in high-volume environments.

In many cases, the largest gains come from redesigning processes rather than replacing labor directly. Automation amplifies the strengths and weaknesses of the underlying system. Well-designed processes benefit from increased efficiency, while poorly designed processes remain constrained even when automated.

Workforce Effects and Skill Demand

Automation changes how work is organized. Tasks that involve repetition and predictability are more likely to be automated, while remaining work increasingly involves supervision, coordination, maintenance, and problem solving.

This shift increases demand for technical skills, including system operation, troubleshooting, and integration. Workers who move into these roles may experience greater stability and higher wages. Workers whose tasks are displaced may face reduced opportunities if they do not have access to training or transition pathways.

The effects are uneven. Automation can reduce physical strain and improve safety in some roles, while increasing uncertainty in others. The availability of training and mobility within the labor market plays a significant role in determining outcomes.

Safety, Standards, and Operational Risk

Safety is central to physical automation. Industrial robots operate with significant force and speed, requiring systems that prevent unintended contact and manage failure conditions. International standards define requirements for safe operation, including system design, risk assessment, and protective measures.[21-04] [21-05]

Safety is not an added feature. It is part of system design and affects layout, workflow, and human interaction. Consistent application of safety standards supports broader adoption by reducing uncertainty and risk.

Automation changes the nature of risk. Manual processes carry risks related to injury, fatigue, and variability. Automated systems reduce some of these risks but introduce others, including system downtime, maintenance requirements, and capital exposure. Managing these risks requires ongoing monitoring, maintenance, and skilled personnel.

Artificial Intelligence and Expanding Capabilities

Advances in artificial intelligence are expanding the range of tasks that can be automated, particularly in perception and motion planning. Systems that rely on machine learning can adapt to variation in ways that were previously difficult to program. Simulation environments allow systems to be trained and tested across a wide range of conditions before deployment.[21-06]

These developments increase flexibility and reduce the time required to deploy new applications. Tasks that previously required tightly controlled conditions can increasingly be performed in more variable environments.

However, physical constraints remain. Real-world environments introduce friction, wear, and uncertainty that cannot be eliminated through software. Reliable automation depends on systems that can operate consistently under these conditions over time.

Economic Structure and Competitive Effects

At a system level, robotics changes how production is organized. Automation can increase output with fewer labor hours, shift work toward higher-skill roles, and alter the geographic distribution of production. Regions that adopt automation more rapidly may improve productivity and competitiveness, particularly in industries where scale and precision are critical.[21-01]

These changes affect supply chains, cost structures, and the location of production. Automation can support reshoring in some cases by reducing labor cost differences, but it also increases the importance of capital investment and technical capability.

The benefits of automation are not evenly distributed. Workers with access to training and technical roles may benefit, while those whose tasks are replaced may face displacement. Firms that deploy automation effectively may gain advantages over those that do not.

Technology, Jobs, and Economic Outcomes

Robotics and physical automation act as a lever within the broader economic system, influencing business decisions about capital investment, labor use, and production design. These decisions shape the number and type of jobs available, the level and stability of income, and the distribution of economic gains.

The impact of automation is not determined by the technology alone, but by how it is integrated into production systems and how changes in work are managed. Systems that use automation to augment human work can increase productivity while maintaining employment pathways. Systems that focus primarily on substitution may increase efficiency but concentrate risk.

The balance between these approaches will determine how automation affects economic stability and mobility over time.

Surveillance and Data Control

Surveillance and data control determine how information about individuals, organizations, and systems is collected, analyzed, and used, shaping decision-making, market power, and the balance between efficiency and autonomy.

Data Collection and Digital Infrastructure

Modern economic systems generate and rely on large volumes of data. Digital platforms, connected devices, financial systems, and public infrastructure continuously collect information about behavior, transactions, location, and performance. This data is often generated as a byproduct of participation in digital systems rather than through explicit collection.

The scale of data collection has expanded rapidly. Estimates suggest that the global volume of data created, captured, and consumed is measured in zettabytes, reflecting exponential growth over the past decade.[21-10] Much of this data is generated through everyday activities, including communication, commerce, navigation, and the use of connected devices.

Data collection is embedded in infrastructure. Sensors, mobile devices, software platforms, and networked systems create a continuous flow of information. Participation in economic and social systems increasingly requires interaction with these data-generating technologies, making data collection a standard feature of modern life.

Data Processing and Decision Systems

The value of data lies in its use. Advances in computing and artificial intelligence allow large datasets to be analyzed and converted into predictions, classifications, and decisions. These systems are used to recommend products, assess risk, allocate resources, and guide operational processes.

Algorithmic decision systems are now used in areas such as credit evaluation, hiring, pricing, and logistics. These systems can process more information and identify patterns more quickly than human decision-makers, increasing efficiency and consistency.[21-11]

At the same time, automated decision systems can embed assumptions and biases present in the data used to train them. Outcomes may be difficult to interpret or challenge, particularly when models are complex or proprietary. The use of automated systems therefore raises questions about transparency, accountability, and oversight.

Data Concentration and Market Power

Control over data can create competitive advantages. Firms that collect and analyze large volumes of data can improve products, optimize operations, and develop new services. As data accumulates, these advantages can increase, creating feedback loops that reinforce market position.

Digital platforms often benefit from network effects, where the value of the service increases as more users participate. Data generated by users improves the system, attracting additional users and generating more data. This dynamic can contribute to market concentration, as larger platforms are better positioned to leverage data at scale.[21-12]

Data concentration can affect competition by raising barriers to entry. New entrants may lack access to comparable data, limiting their ability to develop competing services. Control over data can therefore function as a form of economic power, influencing competition and outcomes.

Surveillance in Commercial and Public Contexts

Surveillance refers to the systematic collection and analysis of information about individuals or groups. In commercial contexts, surveillance is often used to personalize services, target advertising, and manage operations. In public contexts, it may be used for law enforcement, security, and administrative functions.

The distinction between these uses is not always clear. Data collected for one purpose may be used for another, and systems developed in one context may be applied in others. For example, location data used for navigation can also be used for behavioral analysis or monitoring.

The expansion of surveillance capabilities has been enabled by advances in data storage, processing, and sensor technology. Video systems, mobile devices, and networked infrastructure allow for continuous monitoring in both physical and digital environments.[21-13]

These capabilities can improve efficiency and security, but they also raise concerns about privacy, autonomy, and the potential for misuse.

Workplace Monitoring and Labor Management

Surveillance systems are increasingly used in the workplace to monitor performance, track activity, and manage operations. Employers may use software to monitor computer usage, location systems to track movement, and sensors to measure productivity.

These systems can improve efficiency by providing real-time information and enabling more precise management and can also reduce uncertainty in operations and support performance measurement.

However, increased monitoring can change the nature of work. Continuous measurement may reduce autonomy and increase pressure, particularly when performance metrics are closely tied to compensation or job security. Workers may have limited ability to influence how data is collected or used.

The use of surveillance in labor management can therefore shift the balance of control between employers and workers, affecting both working conditions and job satisfaction.

Privacy, Security, and Individual Control

The expansion of data collection raises questions about privacy and individual control. Personal data can include information about identity, behavior, preferences, and location. The ability to collect and analyze this information creates both opportunities and risks.

Data breaches and unauthorized access can expose sensitive information, affecting individuals and organizations. The increasing volume of data stored in digital systems expands the potential impact of such events.[21-14]

Regulatory frameworks have been developed to address these concerns. Laws such as the European Union's General Data Protection Regulation establish requirements for data protection, consent, and individual rights.[21-15] These frameworks aim to balance the benefits of data use with the need to protect individuals from harm.

Despite these efforts, enforcement and compliance vary, and individuals often have limited visibility into how their data is used. Control over personal data is frequently mediated through complex agreements and systems that are not easily understood.

Data as an Economic Asset

Data has become an economic resource. It can be used to improve products, optimize operations, and generate revenue through targeted services and advertising. In some business models, data collection and analysis are central to value creation.

Unlike traditional assets, data can be replicated and reused at low cost. Its value often depends on scale and context, as larger datasets can improve the accuracy and effectiveness of analysis. This can reinforce the advantages of firms that already possess significant data resources.

The economic value of data raises questions about ownership, access, and compensation. Individuals generate data through their activities, but control over that data is often held by the organizations that collect and process it. This creates a separation between data generation and data ownership.

Power, Incentives, and Governance

Surveillance and data control affect the distribution of power within economic systems. Entities that control data can influence decisions, shape behavior, and determine access to information.

Incentives play a central role in how data is used. Firms have incentives to collect and analyze data to improve performance and increase revenue. Governments have incentives to use data for administration and security. Individuals have incentives to use digital services that provide convenience and functionality.

These incentives do not always align. The collection and use of data may create benefits for organizations while imposing costs on individuals, such as reduced privacy or increased monitoring. Governance structures determine how these tradeoffs are managed.

Effective governance requires balancing innovation, efficiency, and protection. This includes defining rights, establishing accountability, and ensuring that the use of data avoids undue harm or concentration of power.

Data, Control, and Economic Outcomes

Surveillance and data control influence economic outcomes by shaping how decisions are made, how markets operate, and how individuals interact with systems. Data-driven decision-making can increase efficiency and improve allocation of resources.

At the same time, concentration of data and control over its use can affect competition, labor conditions, and individual autonomy. Systems that rely heavily on data can centralize decision-making and reduce transparency, particularly when processes are automated or proprietary.

The effects of data control extend beyond individual transactions, shaping markets, the distribution of opportunity, and the balance between efficiency and control.

As data becomes more central to economic activity, the systems that govern its collection and use will play an increasingly important role in determining how benefits and risks are distributed across society.

Economics under AI

As artificial intelligence expands, it changes how work is done and who benefits. The central economic question is not whether productivity will increase, but who governs the consequences when labor, ownership, and decision-making no longer align.

AI and automation are driving structural shifts in economic organization with significant governance implications.

Shifts in Work and Human-Centered Activity

Automation continues to replace routine, repeatable tasks more readily than work requiring judgment, interpersonal interaction, or creativity. As David H. Autor has shown, technological change tends to displace specific tasks rather than entire occupations, while expanding demand for non-routine work that relies on human judgment and interaction.[559]

These patterns are already visible. Employment growth in recent decades has concentrated in both higher-skill and lower-wage service roles, while many middle-skill routine occupations have declined.[560]

At the same time, productivity has continued to rise while wage growth for many workers has slowed. In the United States, labor productivity increased by more than 60 percent between 1979 and 2020, while hourly compensation for typical workers grew by less than 20 percent over the same period.[561] This divergence reflects a growing separation between output and the economic rewards received by labor.

Historically, shifts of this kind have expanded roles in areas such as care, education, design, and service. These activities emphasize creativity, empathy, trust, and social interaction rather than efficiency alone. Whether they become stable sources of livelihood at scale depends less on technology than on how markets, institutions, and compensation systems adapt.

The presence of opportunity does not guarantee accessibility. Transitions are uneven, and the benefits accrue differently depending on education, geography, and existing social support structures.

Structural Changes in Economic Organization

As automation reduces the need for centralized labor and lowers coordination costs, economic organization is shifting away from traditional employment toward more fragmented, task-based forms of participation. Platform-mediated work, contract arrangements, and on-demand services increasingly supplement or replace long-term employment relationships.

This shift changes how risk and responsibility are distributed. Under traditional employment, firms absorbed many forms of uncertainty, including income stability, regulatory compliance, and benefits such as healthcare and retirement. Under task-based and platform-based work, these responsibilities move to individuals.

Estimates suggest that a significant share of the workforce engages in some form of independent or nontraditional work, whether as a primary or supplemental source of income.[562] These arrangements reflect a broader shift in how work is organized.

While these arrangements can increase flexibility, they also introduce income volatility, limited benefits, and reduced access to collective representation.

When contribution replaces employment as the primary measure of value, compensation is tied to discrete outputs or tasks rather than ongoing relationships. Contribution, in this context, refers to work that is assigned, measured, and compensated through transactions rather than continuous employment. This change weakens job-based protections unless intentionally restructured.

Ownership, Concentration, and Distribution

AI-driven productivity tends to concentrate gains among those who control capital, data, and infrastructure rather than among those who supply labor. This dynamic reflects the underlying economics of digital systems, which often involve high fixed costs, low marginal costs, and strong scale advantages.

Once developed, AI systems can be deployed broadly at minimal additional cost. This allows those who control the systems, the data that trains them, and the infrastructure that supports them to capture a disproportionate share of the resulting value.

This pattern is reflected in broader measures of wealth concentration. As already mentioned, in the United States, the top 1 percent of households hold roughly one-third of total wealth, while the bottom half of households hold only a small share.[563] While this concentration predates AI, this new automation reinforces it by reducing the role of labor in value creation.

As ownership becomes more decisive than employment, distribution shifts from wages toward returns on capital, access to ownership, and control over productive systems. How societies respond to that shift is a policy choice, not a technical necessity.

Proposed responses include adjustments to tax structures, expanded access to ownership, public or shared control of certain assets, and revised benefit systems. Each approach involves tradeoffs related to incentives, governance capacity, and legitimacy.

Human Oversight and Decision Authority

A common assumption is that humans will move into supervisory roles as machines perform routine work. While this may occur in some domains, the assumption requires scrutiny.

Authority delegated to automated systems is rarely reclaimed without friction. Once decisions are embedded in algorithms or automated processes, reversing or modifying them can be difficult, particularly when those systems operate at scale.

This is not only a technical issue but a question of control. Delegation of authority reduces direct human oversight, and reclaiming that authority often requires institutional change, regulatory intervention, or system redesign.

Decisions about where human judgment remains decisive, particularly in areas involving allocation, exclusion, or long-term consequences, are governance choices. These decisions determine not only how systems operate, but who is accountable for their outcomes.

The economic impact of AI therefore depends not only on what machines can do, but on who decides how much authority they exercise and under what constraints.

Education, Adaptation, and Time

Economic adaptation to automation is not a one-time event, and it is no longer unfolding slowly. Research suggests that a substantial portion of current work activities could be automated using existing or near-term technologies, though the pace and extent of adoption remain uncertain.[564]

At the same time, populations are aging, and institutions adapt more slowly than technology. This mismatch in speed has become a defining feature of the transition.

Lifelong learning and re-skilling are often proposed as responses, but their effectiveness depends on access, timing, and relevance. Education systems built around early-life credentialing are not well suited to repeated transitions later in life, particularly when change is rapid.

Without structural adjustment, calls for adaptation risk shifting responsibility from institutions to individuals. Whether individuals are expected to bear the cost and risk of adaptation, or whether those responsibilities are shared across institutions, is a governance decision rather than a purely economic outcome.

Measuring Economic Outcomes

Traditional economic indicators such as employment rates and gross domestic product capture only part of the effects of automation. As productivity becomes less dependent on labor, these measures become less reliable indicators of well-being or stability.

An economy can experience rising output while employment stagnates or declines. Digital activity may generate significant value that is not fully reflected in traditional measures, while unpaid or low-paid contributions remain largely uncounted.

Proposals to supplement or revise economic metrics by incorporating factors such as health, environmental sustainability, or public trust reflect these limitations.

Changes in measurement require careful scrutiny. What is counted influences what is rewarded, regulated, or ignored.

Governance, Legitimacy, and Economic Power

The economic effects of AI cannot be separated from governance. Control over automated systems, data, and infrastructure confers power. Whether that power remains accountable depends on legal frameworks, institutional oversight, and public understanding.

Economic outcomes are often presented as the result of technological progress. In practice, they reflect decisions about ownership, regulation, and responsibility.

The legitimacy of an AI-driven economy rests not on efficiency alone, but on whether its rules are transparent, enforceable, and broadly understood. Without that, economic outcomes may become increasingly disconnected from public trust.

Economic Change as a Governance Matter

AI alters economic relationships by shifting where value is created and who controls it. The main challenge is not adaptation to technology, but governance of its effects. A durable economic response to AI supports multiple approaches rather than a single model. It requires clarity about authority, recognition of tradeoffs, and institutions capable of adjusting rules as conditions change.

Technological shifts alter economic structure. Economic structure determines financial power. Financial power shapes governance. As value creation becomes less dependent on labor and more concentrated in capital, data, and infrastructure, control over financial systems becomes increasingly central to how economic power is exercised.

Displacement, Creation, and the Pace of Transition

A central question in the economics of AI is whether job creation will offset job displacement, and over what time frame. Technological change has historically created new forms of work even as it eliminates others, but the timing and distribution of those changes determine whether transitions are manageable or disruptive.

Estimates suggest that a substantial share of current work activities could be automated using existing or near-term technologies. McKinsey has estimated that up to 30 percent of tasks in the global economy could be automated by 2030, with higher exposure in certain occupations and industries.[21-16] These estimates do not imply that jobs disappear entirely, but that significant portions of existing roles may change.

The distinction between tasks and jobs is important, but when tasks change, jobs change with them. When a large share of tasks within a role can be automated, the structure of that role changes. In some cases, remaining tasks can be consolidated into new forms of work. In others, demand for that role declines.

Job creation is influenced by factors beyond technology. New roles emerge when demand exists for new goods, services, or capabilities, and when institutions support transitions. These conditions do not arise automatically but depend on investment, training systems, and the broader economic environment.

The pace of transition is a critical variable. If displacement occurs faster than new roles are created, periods of unemployment or underemployment can increase. If new roles require different skills or are located in different regions, transitions may be uneven and prolonged.

The historical record shows that labor markets can adjust over time, but those adjustments are often uneven and disruptive. The speed of AI adoption, combined with the scale of potential task automation, increases the importance of how transitions are managed.

AI, Productivity, and Wage Distribution

A second question is how the gains from increased productivity are distributed. AI has the potential to increase output by improving efficiency, reducing costs, and enabling new capabilities. However, higher productivity often fails to translate into higher wages.

The relationship between productivity and wages has weakened over time. In the United States, labor productivity has grown substantially since the late twentieth century, while median wage growth has been more limited.[561] This divergence indicates that increases in output are not evenly shared across the workforce.

AI may reinforce this pattern. Digital technologies often allow firms to scale output without a proportional increase in labor. Once developed, AI systems can be deployed across many users or applications at low marginal cost. This allows productivity gains to be captured by those who own the systems rather than those who use them.

Research indicates that automation can have different effects across the wage distribution. It may increase demand for high-skill roles while reducing demand for routine work, contributing to wage polarization.[21-17] At the same time, AI systems can substitute for certain cognitive tasks, potentially affecting occupations that were previously less exposed to automation.

The result can be compression in some parts of the labor market, where workers compete for a narrower set of tasks that remain difficult to automate. Where labor supply exceeds demand, wage growth may slow even as overall productivity increases.

Distribution is influenced by institutional factors, including labor market conditions, bargaining power, and policy. Without mechanisms that link productivity gains to compensation, increases in output may not translate into broad-based income growth.

Ownership, Capital, and the Distribution of Value

As AI systems become more central to production, the distribution of economic value increasingly reflects ownership rather than labor. This shift is driven by the characteristics of digital and automated systems, which involve high initial development costs and low marginal costs of replication.

Firms that control AI models, data, and infrastructure can deploy these systems across a wide range of applications, generating returns that scale with usage. This creates a strong link between ownership and income. Returns accrue to those who own or control the systems, rather than to those who perform the tasks the systems replace.

Empirical evidence suggests that capital income has become a larger share of total income over time, while labor's share has declined in many advanced economies.[21-18] Automation and digitalization contribute to this trend by increasing the relative importance of capital assets, including software, data, and intellectual property.

This shift has implications for wealth distribution. When returns are tied to ownership, individuals and institutions with access to capital can accumulate wealth more rapidly. Those who rely primarily on wages may see slower income growth, particularly if demand for their labor declines.

The concentration of ownership can also affect competition and governance. Firms with significant control over AI systems and data may gain advantages that reinforce their position, increasing barriers to entry and limiting competition.

Responses to these dynamics involve choices about ownership, access, and distribution. Options include expanding access to capital, adjusting tax structures, or establishing shared or public ownership models for certain assets. Each approach involves tradeoffs related to incentives, efficiency, and governance capacity.

As value creation becomes more closely tied to capital, data, and infrastructure, the distribution of economic outcomes depends increasingly on who owns and controls those resources, and on the rules that govern their use.

SECTION VI — Economic Outcomes and Feedback

Measurable Outcomes

Economic systems ultimately produce outcomes that can be observed in behavior, health, stability, and social cohesion, providing measurable indicators of how effectively those systems translate resources and incentives into broad-based well-being.

Crime and Economic Conditions

Crime reflects both individual behavior and broader economic and social conditions. While criminal activity is influenced by many factors, including law enforcement practices and demographic trends, economic stability, employment opportunities, and income distribution are consistently associated with variations in crime rates.

Periods of economic distress have often been linked to increases in certain types of crime, particularly property crimes. When legitimate opportunities for income are limited, the relative incentives for illegal activity can change. Research has found that higher unemployment and lower wages are associated with increased rates of property crime, though the relationship is not uniform across all categories.[22-01]

Violent crime follows a more complex pattern, influenced by factors such as social cohesion, exposure to violence, and access to weapons. However, long-term trends show that communities with persistent poverty and limited economic opportunity often experience higher rates of violent crime.[22-02]

Recent data indicate that overall violent crime rates in the United States increased sharply during 2020 and 2021 before declining in subsequent years, illustrating how rapidly conditions can shift.22-03 Crime rates vary significantly across regions, reflecting differences in economic conditions, policing strategies, and community structures.

Crime imposes both direct and indirect costs. Direct costs include losses to victims and expenditures on law enforcement and incarceration. Indirect costs include reduced investment, lower property values, and diminished quality of life. These effects can reinforce economic disadvantage in affected communities.

The relationship between economic systems and crime is therefore not only a matter of enforcement, but of opportunity. Systems that provide stable employment, predictable income, and pathways for advancement tend to reduce the conditions associated with higher crime rates, while systems that generate instability or exclusion may increase them.

Mental Health and Economic Stress

Mental health is closely linked to economic conditions. Income stability, employment security, and access to healthcare influence psychological well-being, while economic uncertainty can contribute to stress, anxiety, and depression.

Data from national surveys indicate that a significant share of adults report symptoms of anxiety or depressive disorders, with higher prevalence among individuals facing financial strain or job instability.[22-04] Economic downturns have been associated with increases in mental health challenges, including higher rates of depression and substance use.[22-05]

Work conditions also play a role. Jobs characterized by high demands and low control are associated with increased stress and negative health outcomes. Income volatility, irregular schedules, and job insecurity can further contribute to psychological strain.

Mental health outcomes have broader economic effects. Reduced well-being can affect productivity, labor force participation, and healthcare costs. Individuals experiencing mental health challenges may have difficulty maintaining employment or pursuing opportunities for advancement, reinforcing economic disparities.

At a system level, mental health reflects the interaction between economic structure and individual experience. Stable conditions, access to services, and supportive environments can mitigate stress, while instability and limited access can exacerbate it.

Dependency and Economic Support Systems

Dependency refers to reliance on external support for income, whether through public assistance, private transfers, or informal support networks. The structure of economic systems influences both the need for support and the forms it takes.

Public assistance programs provide support for individuals who are unemployed, disabled, or unable to meet basic needs. Participation in these programs varies with economic conditions, increasing during periods of downturn and declining as employment opportunities expand.[22-06]

Long-term reliance on assistance can reflect structural factors such as limited job opportunities, health constraints, or skill mismatches. It can also be influenced by program design, including eligibility criteria and benefit structures, which shape incentives to work.

At the same time, support systems can provide stability and prevent more severe outcomes, including poverty, homelessness, and health crises. The presence of safety nets can reduce the impact of economic shocks and support transitions back into employment.

The relationship between dependency and economic systems is therefore complex. Systems that generate stable employment and income reduce reliance on support, while systems that produce volatility or exclusion increase it. The design of support programs influences whether they function primarily as temporary assistance or as long-term income sources.

Social Stability and Breakdown Indicators

Broader measures of social stability provide additional insight into economic outcomes. Indicators such as family structure, community engagement, substance use, and mortality rates reflect underlying social conditions that are influenced by economic systems.

In the United States, changes in family formation, including declines in marriage rates and increases in single-parent households, have been associated with economic factors such as income instability and employment prospects.[22-07]

Substance use and overdose deaths have increased significantly in recent decades, with opioid-related deaths reaching historically high levels.[22-08] These trends are often concentrated in regions experiencing economic decline and are influenced by multiple factors, including healthcare practices and access to treatment.

Mortality patterns also reflect broader social conditions. Increases in deaths related to suicide, drug overdose, and alcohol have been described as "deaths of despair," particularly among certain demographic groups.[22-09] These patterns are associated with economic dislocation, loss of stable employment, and reduced social cohesion.

Social indicators do not move independently of economic conditions. Changes in employment, income stability, and opportunity can influence family formation, health behaviors, and community engagement. Over time, these effects accumulate, shaping broader patterns of stability or fragmentation.

Outcomes as System Feedback

Measures such as crime, mental health, dependency, and social stability function as feedback mechanisms within economic systems, reflecting how incentives, opportunities, and constraints are experienced at the individual and community level.

When systems provide stable pathways to income and advancement, outcomes tend to reflect higher levels of participation and stability. When systems produce volatility, exclusion, or concentrated disadvantage, outcomes may reflect increased stress, reduced opportunity, and greater reliance on support.

These indicators do not provide simple answers, but they offer measurable signals of system performance. Changes in these measures can indicate whether economic structures are producing broadly shared benefits or contributing to instability.

Understanding these outcomes requires linking economic conditions to lived experience. The effectiveness of an economic system is not determined solely by output or efficiency, but by how those outputs translate into stability, opportunity, and well-being across the population.

Economic Classes and Social Stability

Economic systems distribute not only income, but also opportunity, risk, and security. Over time, those distributions shape social structure and influence stability across the population.

Income, Wealth, and Economic Position

Groups form not by ideology alone, but by their position within the economy, including their access to income, assets, and stability. These structural differences influence how people experience economic change and how they respond to it.

A key distinction is between income and wealth. Income reflects earnings over time, typically through work. Wealth reflects accumulated assets such as savings, investments, property, and ownership stakes. Income supports current living standards, while wealth provides resilience. Those with assets can absorb shocks, invest in opportunities, and pass advantages to the next generation. Those without assets are more exposed to disruption and less able to recover from setbacks.

The distribution of wealth in the United States is highly concentrated. The top 1 percent of households hold more than 30 percent of total wealth, while the bottom 50 percent hold only a small share, often estimated at around 2 percent.[22-10] This concentration means that a large portion of the population relies primarily on income rather than accumulated assets, making them more vulnerable to economic fluctuations.

Stability, Risk, and Economic Security

Differences in wealth translate into differences in stability. Households with substantial assets can withstand periods of unemployment, invest in education or relocation, and benefit from long-term market gains. Households without such resources face tighter constraints. Job loss, health expenses, or unexpected costs can quickly lead to financial distress, limiting mobility and increasing dependence on external support.

Financial fragility reflects this gap. Survey data indicate that a significant share of households would have difficulty covering an unexpected expense without borrowing or selling assets.[22-11] Limited savings increase exposure to short-term shocks and reduce the ability to plan for long-term opportunities.

As work becomes more flexible and income more variable, differences in savings, income stability, and access to assets can widen. When employment becomes less stable and benefits shift from employers to individuals, those without assets must absorb greater risk. Income volatility, limited savings, and rising costs can compound over time, reducing the ability to move upward economically. In contrast, those with capital can benefit from returns on investment even as labor conditions become less predictable.

Mobility, Opportunity, and Economic Pathways

Economic stability is closely tied to mobility. The ability to move between income levels depends on access to education, employment opportunities, and capital. When pathways for advancement are accessible, differences in income and wealth may be viewed as transitional. When those pathways narrow, disparities become more persistent.

Research on intergenerational mobility indicates that outcomes vary significantly by geography and background. In some regions, individuals born into lower-income households have a higher probability of moving upward, while in others mobility is more limited.[22-12] These differences reflect variations in education systems, labor markets, and social conditions.

Access to opportunity is not evenly distributed. Differences in education, location, and social networks can affect the ability to acquire skills, find employment, and build assets. Over time, these factors contribute to the persistence of economic classes across generations.

Concentration, Distribution, and Social Tension

Economic structure influences social stability. When large segments of the population experience limited mobility, persistent insecurity, or declining real opportunity, dissatisfaction can increase. Historical and empirical studies show that sustained disparities in wealth and income are associated with higher levels of social tension and reduced institutional trust.[22-13]

The issue is not inequality alone, but whether the economic system provides a credible path for advancement. When individuals believe that effort can lead to improvement, disparities are more likely to be accepted as temporary or earned. When that path narrows or becomes uncertain, the system is more likely to be viewed as fixed or unresponsive.

These perceptions influence behavior. Reduced trust in institutions, lower civic participation, and increased polarization can emerge when economic outcomes are perceived as uneven or inaccessible. Social stability depends not only on absolute levels of income, but on how those outcomes are distributed and understood.

Policy, Capital Allocation, and Work Structure

Economic policy, labor markets, and technological change shape how opportunity is distributed and how risks are shared. Decisions about taxation, education, work structure, and access to capital influence whether economic gains are broadly accessible or increasingly concentrated.

Work is not independent. It reflects how capital is allocated, how markets are structured, and how incentives are set. Policies governing taxation, credit, regulation, and trade determine where capital flows, which industries expand or contract, and how risk is distributed.

These forces appear in job design, the availability of jobs, and the stability of income across the population. When capital flows primarily toward sectors that require limited labor or concentrate returns, employment opportunities may narrow. When investment supports broader participation, opportunities may expand.

Economic Structure and Social Stability

When opportunity compresses, stability declines. Economic systems that limit mobility and concentrate risk among those least able to bear it create conditions that can weaken social cohesion over time.

Economic classes are not fixed categories, but they reflect patterns of access, stability, and opportunity that persist across time. Understanding these patterns provides a foundation for examining how financial systems, corporate organization, and public policy interact in shaping long-term outcomes.

The relationship between economic structure and social stability is not indirect. It is a direct outcome of how income, wealth, and opportunity are distributed, and of whether those distributions allow for movement, security, and participation across the population.

Inequality and Distribution

Inequality and distribution describe how income, wealth, and economic gains are allocated across a population, shaping opportunity, incentives, and long-term system stability.

Income Distribution and Earnings

Income distribution reflects how earnings are spread across households and individuals. It is influenced by wages, employment structure, education, and labor market conditions. Changes in income distribution affect living standards, consumption, and the ability to invest in future opportunities.

In the United States, income inequality has increased over several decades. Measures such as the Gini coefficient indicate a widening dispersion of income, with higher-income households capturing a larger share of total earnings.[22-14] At the same time, real wage growth for many middle- and lower-income workers has been slower than overall economic growth, contributing to divergence in living standards.

Differences in income are shaped by both market forces and institutional factors. Technological change, globalization, and shifts in labor demand can increase returns to certain skills. Policies related to taxation, minimum wages, and labor protections also influence how income is distributed.

Income distribution is not static. It reflects ongoing interactions between economic conditions, policy decisions, and labor market dynamics.

Wealth Distribution and Asset Ownership

Wealth distribution differs from income distribution in both scale and persistence. Wealth accumulates over time and can be transferred across generations, reinforcing existing advantages.

In the United States, wealth is more concentrated than income. The top 1 percent of households hold a large share of total wealth, while many households hold limited assets.22-10 This concentration affects economic security, as wealth provides a buffer against shocks and a source of investment capital.

Asset ownership influences access to opportunity. Households with financial assets, property, or business ownership can benefit from market growth, while those without assets rely primarily on income. Differences in ownership therefore contribute to differences in long-term outcomes.

Changes in asset values, including housing and financial markets, can further affect distribution. When asset prices rise, those who hold assets benefit, while those who do not may face higher barriers to entry.

Returns to Capital and Labor

The distribution of income depends in part on the relative returns to capital and labor. When returns to capital increase relative to wages, a larger share of economic gains accrues to asset owners.

Research indicates that in many advanced economies, the share of income going to labor has declined over time, while returns to capital have increased.[22-15] This shift reflects changes in technology, competition, and globalization, which can increase the importance of capital-intensive production.

Digital and automated systems can amplify this trend. Once developed, these systems can be scaled at low marginal cost, allowing returns to be concentrated among those who control the underlying assets. This can increase disparities if ownership is concentrated.

The balance between capital and labor is influenced by policy, market competition, and institutional arrangements. Changes in this balance affect both income distribution and broader economic stability.

Regional and Sectoral Differences

Inequality is not uniform across regions or sectors. Economic activity is concentrated in certain areas, often those with access to infrastructure, education, and capital. This concentration can lead to differences in income, employment opportunities, and growth rates across regions.

Urban areas with strong labor markets and high levels of investment may experience rising incomes and asset values, while other regions may face slower growth. These differences can contribute to geographic disparities in opportunity and living standards.

Sectoral differences also matter. Industries that benefit from technological change or global demand may generate higher wages and returns, while others may experience stagnation or decline. Workers in declining sectors may face limited opportunities for transition, particularly if skills are not easily transferable.

These regional and sectoral variations contribute to the overall pattern of inequality and influence migration, investment, and policy priorities.

Distribution, Opportunity, and System Stability

The effects of inequality depend not only on its level, but on its structure and persistence. Systems with high inequality can remain stable if pathways for advancement are accessible and widely perceived as fair. When mobility is limited and disparities persist across generations, stability may weaken.

Inequality can influence incentives. Differences in income and wealth can motivate effort and investment, but large or persistent disparities can reduce participation if individuals perceive opportunities as limited.

Economic outcomes are also linked to social conditions. High levels of inequality have been associated with differences in health, education, and social cohesion.[22-13] These relationships are complex and influenced by multiple factors, but they reflect the broader impact of distribution on society.

The balance between efficiency and distribution is a central issue in economic systems. Policies that affect taxation, education, labor markets, and access to capital all influence how economic gains are distributed.

Distribution as a System Outcome

Inequality is not a single outcome. It is the result of how systems allocate resources, define incentives, and distribute risk. It reflects decisions about ownership, compensation, and access to opportunity.

Changes in distribution signal underlying shifts in economic structure. When gains are broadly shared, income and wealth tend to grow across a wider segment of the population. When gains are concentrated, disparities increase.

Understanding inequality requires examining both market outcomes and institutional frameworks. Distribution is shaped not only by economic activity, but by the rules that govern that activity.

As economic systems evolve, the distribution of income and wealth remains a central factor in determining stability, opportunity, and long-term outcomes.

Economic Mobility

Economic mobility reflects the ability of individuals and households to improve their economic position over time, shaping whether effort, skill, and opportunity translate into advancement within a given system.

Absolute and Relative Mobility

Mobility can be measured in two ways. Absolute mobility refers to whether individuals earn more than their parents in real terms. Relative mobility refers to movement within the income distribution, such as moving from a lower income group to a higher one.

In the United States, both measures have changed over time. Research indicates that the share of children earning more than their parents has declined significantly over the past several decades. For those born in 1940, more than 90 percent earned more than their parents, while for those born in the 1980s, the share is closer to 50 percent.[22-12] This decline reflects slower income growth and changes in distribution.

Relative mobility also varies across populations. Movement between income levels is possible, but it is uneven. Individuals born into higher-income households are more likely to remain in higher income positions, while those born into lower-income households face greater barriers to upward movement.

These patterns indicate that mobility is not solely determined by individual effort. Structural conditions influence the likelihood of advancement.

Intergenerational Persistence and Opportunity

Economic outcomes are often linked across generations. Income, wealth, education, and social networks can be transmitted from parents to children, affecting future opportunities.

Children from higher-income households are more likely to have access to resources that support advancement, including education, stable environments, and financial support. These factors can influence long-term outcomes, including earnings and occupational status.

Conversely, children from lower-income households may face constraints that limit access to these resources. Differences in school quality, neighborhood conditions, and exposure to economic instability can affect development and opportunity.

Advantages and disadvantages often carry across generations, concentrating opportunity. When resources, education, and networks pass from parents to children, mobility is more common among those already positioned to advance.

Geography, Education, and Access

Mobility varies significantly by geography. Research has shown that the probability of upward mobility differs across regions, with some areas providing greater opportunities for advancement than others. Factors associated with higher mobility include access to quality education, lower levels of segregation, and stronger labor markets.[22-16]

Education is a key pathway for mobility, but its effectiveness depends on access, quality, and cost. Higher levels of education are generally associated with higher earnings, but the returns to education vary by field of study and labor market conditions.

Rising costs of education can create barriers to access, particularly for individuals without financial resources. Student debt can also affect long-term financial outcomes, influencing decisions related to employment, housing, and investment.

Geographic and educational factors interact. Access to quality education often depends on location, and relocation may be constrained by housing costs and economic resources. These interactions contribute to differences in mobility across populations.

Labor Markets and Mobility Pathways

Labor market conditions play a central role in mobility. The availability of stable, well-paying jobs provides a pathway for advancement, while limited opportunities can constrain movement.

Changes in how work is organized affect these pathways. The decline of some middle-skill occupations and the growth of both high-skill and lower-wage service jobs have altered the distribution of opportunities. Workers may face transitions that require new skills or relocation, which are not equally accessible to all.

Wage growth and job stability influence the ability to move upward. When wages stagnate or employment is unstable, individuals may find it more difficult to accumulate savings, invest in education, or pursue new opportunities.

Mobility also depends on entry points. Access to initial employment opportunities, including internships, apprenticeships, and entry-level roles, can affect long-term outcomes. Barriers at these stages can limit upward movement over time.

Wealth, Risk, and Financial Resilience

Wealth plays a significant role in mobility by providing a buffer against risk. Individuals with savings or assets can take actions that support advancement, such as pursuing education, relocating, or starting a business.

Those without assets face greater constraints. Financial shocks, such as job loss or health expenses, can disrupt progress and limit future opportunities. Limited access to credit can further restrict the ability to invest in advancement.

Differences in wealth therefore affect not only current stability, but future mobility. When access to capital is uneven, opportunities for advancement may be similarly uneven.

These dynamics reinforce the link between wealth distribution and mobility. Concentrated wealth can lead to concentrated opportunity, while limited access to assets can constrain movement.

Perception, Incentives, and Participation

Perceptions of mobility influence behavior. When individuals believe that effort can lead to advancement, they may be more likely to invest in education, seek opportunities, and participate in economic activity.

When mobility is perceived as limited or inaccessible, incentives may weaken. Individuals may reduce investment in skills or disengage from pathways that appear unlikely to lead to improvement.

These perceptions are shaped by both experience and information. Observed outcomes within communities, as well as broader narratives about opportunity, influence expectations.

Participation in economic systems depends not only on actual opportunities, but on whether those opportunities are perceived as attainable.

Mobility and System Stability

Economic mobility is a key component of system stability. Systems that allow movement across income levels can accommodate differences in outcomes while maintaining legitimacy. When mobility is limited, disparities may become more entrenched, increasing the risk of dissatisfaction.

Mobility affects how inequality is experienced. High levels of inequality may be more stable if mobility is strong, while even moderate inequality may generate tension if mobility is limited.

Policies that affect education, labor markets, housing, and access to capital all influence mobility. These policies shape whether opportunities for advancement are broadly available or concentrated.

Mobility is not only an economic outcome, but a reflection of how systems distribute opportunity over time. Its presence or absence influences participation, expectations, and long-term stability.

Institutional Trust

Institutional trust reflects the extent to which individuals believe that economic, political, and social institutions operate fairly, predictably, and in the public interest, shaping participation, compliance, and long-term system stability.

Trust in Economic and Financial Institutions

Trust in economic institutions affects how individuals engage with markets. Banks, financial systems, employers, and regulatory bodies depend on confidence to function effectively. When individuals trust that contracts will be honored, that systems are stable, and that rules are applied consistently, participation increases.

Survey data indicate that trust in financial institutions varies over time, often declining following periods of crisis and recovering gradually as conditions stabilize.[22-17] The financial crisis of 2008, for example, was associated with a significant decline in trust in banks and financial markets, reflecting concerns about risk, accountability, and oversight.

Trust influences behavior. Individuals are more likely to invest, save, and engage in financial markets when they believe systems are reliable. When trust is low, participation may decline, and individuals may rely more on informal or alternative systems.

The functioning of economic systems therefore depends not only on performance, but on the perceived legitimacy of institutions.

Government, Policy, and Public Confidence

Trust in government institutions shapes how policies are received and implemented. When individuals believe that governments act in the public interest and apply rules consistently, compliance is more likely. When trust declines, resistance to policy and reduced engagement can follow.

Long-term survey data show that trust in government in the United States has declined from levels observed in the mid-twentieth century, with a smaller share of the population expressing confidence in federal institutions.[22-18] These changes reflect a combination of factors, including political polarization, economic conditions, and perceptions of effectiveness.

Public confidence is influenced by outcomes. Policies that are perceived as fair and effective can reinforce trust, while perceived failures or inconsistencies can weaken it. Transparency, accountability, and responsiveness play central roles in maintaining confidence.

Trust also affects policy capacity. Governments rely on voluntary compliance in areas such as taxation and regulation. Lower trust can increase enforcement costs and reduce the effectiveness of policy interventions.

Information, Transparency, and Perception

Institutional trust depends on access to information and the ability to evaluate it. Transparency allows individuals to understand how decisions are made and to assess whether institutions are operating as intended.

The expansion of digital media has increased the availability of information, but it has also introduced challenges related to accuracy and verification. The volume of information can make it difficult to distinguish between reliable and unreliable sources.

Perceptions of fairness and competence are shaped not only by outcomes, but by how information is presented and interpreted. Conflicting narratives and misinformation can affect trust, even when underlying systems remain unchanged.

Institutions that provide clear, consistent, and verifiable information are more likely to maintain trust. When information is limited, inconsistent, or perceived as biased, confidence may decline.

Fairness, Consistency, and Rule Enforcement

Trust is closely linked to perceptions of fairness and consistency. Individuals are more likely to trust institutions when rules are applied equally and outcomes are predictable.

Inconsistent enforcement or perceived preferential treatment can reduce trust. When similar situations produce different outcomes, individuals may question whether systems are fair or influenced by factors unrelated to merit or rules.

Fairness also relates to process. Transparent procedures, clear standards, and opportunities for review or appeal can reinforce confidence, even when outcomes are not favorable to all participants.

Institutions that maintain consistent rules and clear processes are better able to sustain trust over time. Variability in application or outcomes can undermine confidence, particularly when it affects large segments of the population.

Economic Outcomes and Trust Formation

Economic conditions influence trust in institutions. Stable employment, rising incomes, and accessible opportunities can reinforce confidence in systems. Conversely, periods of instability, limited mobility, or concentrated gains may weaken trust.

Research indicates that trust in institutions is associated with economic performance, though the relationship is complex.[22-19] Positive economic outcomes can support trust, while perceived inequities or persistent disparities can reduce it.

Trust is also influenced by distribution. When economic gains are broadly shared, institutions may be viewed as more legitimate. When gains are concentrated, perceptions of fairness may decline, particularly if opportunities for advancement are limited.

The interaction between economic outcomes and trust creates feedback effects. Trust can support economic activity, while economic conditions can influence trust, reinforcing or weakening the system over time.

Trust, Participation, and Compliance

Institutional trust affects participation in economic and social systems. Individuals who trust institutions are more likely to comply with regulations, pay taxes, and engage in civic processes.

Lower trust can lead to reduced participation or increased reliance on alternative systems. Informal economies, reduced tax compliance, and disengagement from civic institutions can emerge when trust is limited.

Compliance is not only a matter of enforcement. It is also influenced by legitimacy. When individuals perceive rules as fair and institutions as credible, compliance is more likely to occur voluntarily.

This relationship affects the cost of governance. Systems with higher trust can rely more on voluntary compliance, while those with lower trust may require greater enforcement and oversight.

Institutional Trust and System Stability

Institutional trust is a central component of system stability. It affects how individuals respond to economic and political changes and whether they accept outcomes as legitimate.

Systems with higher levels of trust are better able to adapt to change. Individuals are more likely to accept temporary disruptions if they believe that institutions are functioning effectively and fairly. When trust is low, similar disruptions may generate stronger negative reactions.

Trust also affects the ability to implement long-term policies. Investments in infrastructure, education, or environmental sustainability often require sustained commitment. Trust supports this commitment by reinforcing confidence in future outcomes.

When trust declines, the capacity for coordinated action may weaken. This can affect both economic performance and social cohesion.

Trust as a System Outcome

Institutional trust is not fixed. It is an outcome of how systems perform, how decisions are made, and how those decisions are communicated.

Trust reflects the alignment between expectations and outcomes. When institutions operate in ways that are perceived as fair, transparent, and effective, trust tends to increase. When there is a gap between expectations and outcomes, trust may decline.

As economic systems evolve, maintaining institutional trust requires attention to both performance and perception. The legitimacy of institutions depends not only on their ability to produce results, but on whether those results are understood and accepted by the population.

Political Pressure and Feedback

Economic outcomes generate political pressure, and political systems respond through feedback mechanisms that adjust policy, redistribute resources, and reshape institutional authority over time.

Economic Conditions and Political Response

Economic conditions influence political behavior. Changes in employment, income, and stability affect how individuals evaluate policies and institutions. When economic outcomes are stable and broadly distributed, political pressure tends to be lower. When outcomes are uneven or uncertain, pressure for change increases.

Voting patterns, policy preferences, and public engagement are often linked to economic experience. Individuals and groups that experience economic decline or limited mobility may seek changes in policy, while those benefiting from existing conditions may favor continuity. These differences shape political alignment and policy debates.

Economic shocks can accelerate political response. Periods of recession, rapid inflation, or structural change can lead to shifts in policy priorities and political outcomes. These responses may include changes in fiscal policy, regulation, or institutional structure.

The relationship between economic conditions and political behavior is not uniform, but economic experience remains a central factor in shaping political response.

Distribution, Representation, and Policy Influence

The distribution of economic resources affects political influence. Individuals and organizations with greater financial resources may have more capacity to participate in political processes, including funding campaigns, supporting advocacy, and influencing policy discussions.

Research indicates that policy outcomes are often more closely aligned with the preferences of higher-income individuals and organized interest groups than with those of the broader population.[22-20] This relationship reflects differences in access, organization, and participation.

Representation is influenced by both formal structures and informal dynamics. Voting systems, districting, and institutional design shape how preferences are translated into policy. At the same time, lobbying, campaign financing, and media influence can affect which issues receive attention and how they are addressed.

These dynamics do not eliminate democratic participation, but they affect how influence is distributed. The degree to which policy reflects a broad range of interests is a function of both institutional design and economic structure.

Feedback Loops and Policy Adjustment

Political systems incorporate feedback mechanisms that respond to economic outcomes. Elections, legislative processes, and administrative actions allow for adjustments in policy over time.

Feedback can operate through multiple channels. Public opinion, economic indicators, and institutional performance all influence policy decisions. When outcomes are perceived as unsatisfactory, pressure for change can lead to policy revisions.

However, feedback is not always immediate or proportional. Institutional constraints, political incentives, and information limitations can delay or distort responses. Policies may persist even when outcomes change, particularly if adjustment requires coordination or involves competing interests.

Feedback loops can also reinforce existing conditions. Policies that benefit certain groups may increase their capacity to influence future decisions, while groups with less influence may have limited ability to affect outcomes. This can lead to persistence in both policy and economic structure.

Polarization and Policy Divergence

Differences in economic experience can contribute to political polarization. When groups experience different outcomes or perceive different opportunities, their policy preferences may diverge.

Polarization can affect the ability of political systems to respond to economic conditions. Divergent preferences may lead to disagreement over policy direction, reducing the likelihood of coordinated action. This can delay responses to economic challenges or result in partial or temporary measures.

Polarization is influenced by multiple factors, including economic conditions, information environments, and institutional structures. Economic disparities can contribute to differences in perspective, but they interact with broader social and political dynamics.

The interaction between economic conditions and political polarization affects both policy outcomes and system stability.

Institutional Capacity and Constraints

The ability of political systems to respond to economic conditions depends on institutional capacity. This includes the ability to design, implement, and enforce policies effectively.

Institutional capacity is influenced by resources, expertise, and organizational structure. It is also affected by legal and procedural constraints, which can limit the range of available actions or the speed of response.

Constraints can provide stability by preventing rapid or unpredictable changes, but they can also limit adaptability. When economic conditions change quickly, institutions may face challenges in responding effectively within existing frameworks.

The balance between stability and adaptability is a key aspect of governance. Systems that are too rigid may struggle to adjust, while systems that are too flexible may lack predictability.

Legitimacy, Outcomes, and System Stability

Political systems depend on legitimacy, which is influenced by both processes and outcomes. When individuals believe that institutions operate fairly and produce acceptable results, legitimacy is reinforced. When outcomes are perceived as unfair or processes as ineffective, legitimacy may decline.

Economic outcomes play a central role in this process. Persistent disparities, limited mobility, or economic instability can affect perceptions of fairness and effectiveness. These perceptions influence participation, compliance, and support for institutions.

Legitimacy is not static. It evolves as conditions change and as institutions respond. Maintaining legitimacy requires alignment between expectations, processes, and outcomes.

Political Feedback as a System Mechanism

Political pressure and feedback link economic outcomes to policy decisions, providing a mechanism through which systems adjust to changing conditions.

This process is not purely reactive. Political decisions also shape economic outcomes, creating a continuous interaction between economic and political systems. Policies influence incentives, resource allocation, and distribution, which in turn affect future political responses.

The effectiveness of this feedback mechanism depends on the responsiveness and capacity of institutions. Systems that can incorporate feedback and adjust policies are better able to maintain stability. Systems that do not respond effectively may experience increasing pressure over time.

SECTION VII — Reform

Consumer Protection and Corporations

Modern markets concentrate scale, information, and leverage within firms, while individual consumers often lack the expertise and bargaining power to evaluate risk, creating conditions in which oversight becomes a mechanism for maintaining trust and stability.

Market Power, Information, and Consumer Limits

Even where markets function competitively, individual consumers often lack the information and leverage needed to protect their interests. Large corporations operate with legal teams, data analytics, supply chain control, and marketing capabilities that no individual consumer can realistically match. In theory, consumer choice provides protection. In practice, choice is often constrained by information gaps, product complexity, and unequal bargaining power.[23-18]

Markets reward efficiency and innovation, but they also tend to concentrate power. As firms scale, they can control pricing, product design, and distribution in ways that are not fully visible to consumers. When power concentrates faster than accountability mechanisms evolve, the risk of harm increases.[23-19]

The issue is not whether markets create value, but whether they can reliably prevent harm when consumers lack the ability to evaluate risk. This imbalance has led to the development of consumer protection institutions designed to address information asymmetry and enforce minimum standards.

The Consumer Product Safety Commission

Congress created the Consumer Product Safety Commission in 1972 to protect the public from unreasonable risks associated with consumer products.[23-14] The agency was formed in response to widespread injuries and deaths linked to unsafe household goods, toys, appliances, and other widely distributed products.[23-01, 23-15]

Before the CPSC, product safety oversight was fragmented and largely reactive. Manufacturers were often responsible for safety unless negligence could be proven in court, placing the burden on injured consumers after harm occurred. The CPSC shifted this approach toward prevention. It was granted authority to establish safety standards, require testing, mandate recalls, and collect injury data to identify patterns of risk.[23-16]

The need for centralized oversight reflects the nature of modern production. Consumers cannot independently evaluate the structural integrity of a crib, the flammability of a mattress, or the electrical safety of an appliance. These risks are embedded in design and manufacturing processes that are not visible at the point of purchase.

Critics argue that regulatory agencies can impose excessive compliance costs, discourage smaller producers, and slow innovation. These concerns reflect the tradeoff between safety and efficiency. Maintaining effective oversight requires standards that are evidence-based, transparent, and proportionate to risk.

The absence of oversight also carries costs. Unsafe products can lead to injury, medical expenses, and broader public health consequences. The CPSC represents an institutional effort to balance innovation with accountability in markets where harm can scale across large populations.

The Consumer Financial Protection Bureau

The Consumer Financial Protection Bureau was established in 2010 following the 2007 to 2008 financial crisis. While the CPSC focuses on physical goods, the CFPB regulates financial products, including mortgages, credit cards, student loans, and consumer lending.

Financial products often involve complex terms that are difficult to evaluate. Fees, interest structures, and contractual conditions can be layered in ways that obscure risk. In the period leading up to the financial crisis, mortgage products and related financial instruments were frequently sold with terms that many borrowers did not fully understand, contributing to systemic risk.[23-02,23-17]

The CFPB consolidated consumer financial oversight that had previously been distributed across multiple agencies. Its mandate includes enforcing fair lending laws, preventing deceptive practices, supervising financial institutions, and improving transparency in consumer contracts.

Supporters view the CFPB as a counterbalance to large financial institutions with greater resources and technical expertise than individual borrowers. Critics argue that its structure concentrates authority and may impose compliance burdens that restrict credit or limit innovation. Legal challenges have focused on the scope of its authority and its independence from traditional appropriations processes.[23-03]

These debates reflect broader questions about the role of administrative agencies in regulating complex markets.

Information Asymmetry and Market Outcomes

Both the CPSC and the CFPB address a common structural issue. Consumers often lack access to the information needed to evaluate products and services, while firms possess detailed knowledge of design, risk, and performance.

In competitive markets, price and quality can signal value, but they do not always reveal hidden risks. Hazards may be embedded in manufacturing processes or contract terms that are not apparent to buyers. Without mechanisms to collect data, enforce standards, and correct failures, these risks may only become visible after harm occurs.

Information asymmetry can affect market outcomes. When consumers cannot distinguish between safer and riskier products, incentives for firms to invest in safety or transparency may weaken. Oversight can help align incentives by establishing minimum standards and increasing accountability.

The effectiveness of these mechanisms depends on the quality of information, the clarity of rules, and the consistency of enforcement.

Regulation, Incentives, and Accountability

Regulatory agencies operate within statutory frameworks defined by Congress. Oversight, judicial review, and legislative processes provide mechanisms for accountability and adjustment. These constraints are intended to balance the need for regulation with limits on administrative authority.

Regulation affects incentives. Clear and consistent rules can support investment by reducing uncertainty, while excessive or inconsistent regulation can increase costs and discourage innovation. The challenge is to design systems that protect consumers without unnecessarily restricting economic activity.

Accountability operates in both directions. Firms are accountable for product safety and fair practices, while regulators are accountable for the scope and effectiveness of their actions. This balance is central to maintaining both market efficiency and public confidence.

Trust, Markets, and System Stability

Market stability depends in part on trust. Consumers must have confidence that products are reasonably safe and that financial agreements are not structured to deceive. Without this confidence, participation may decline, and reliance on formal markets may weaken.

Consumer protection institutions aim to preserve that trust by narrowing the gap between corporate capability and individual vulnerability, establishing conditions under which markets can function more reliably without replacing them.

These issues extend beyond individual transactions, affecting how systems manage risk, distribute responsibility, and maintain legitimacy. When consumers believe that markets are fair and that protections are in place, participation increases. When trust declines, economic and social stability can be affected.

Consumer protection reflects a broader principle. As systems become more complex and power becomes more concentrated, the mechanisms that ensure accountability become more central to maintaining both efficiency and stability.

Taxes as Control

Corporate Personhood

Corporate personhood reflects how economic power is exercised through organizations rather than individuals, raising fundamental issues about rights, accountability, and democratic balance.

Corporations in the United States are treated like individuals regarding certain legal rights. This treatment is based on the legal concept of corporate personhood. Corporate personhood means that a corporation, as a legal entity, can enter into contracts, sue and be sued, own assets, and pay taxes. This concept has been part of U.S. law since the 19th century but gained significant attention from the Supreme Court's 2010 decision in *Citizens United v. Federal Election Commission* (2010). In that case, the Court ruled that corporations have a First Amendment right to free speech, which includes the right to spend money on political campaigning. This decision affirmed the idea that corporations can exercise some of the same legal rights as individuals, particularly regarding political speech. This decision affirmed the legality of corporate political spending, which critics argue can increase corporate influence relative to individual citizens' access to their representatives.

While corporations in the United States are granted certain rights similar to individuals, they do not possess all the rights that natural persons do. Corporations cannot vote in elections, register for Social Security, obtain driver's licenses, or serve in the military. Their privacy rights are also more limited; business premises may be subject to regulatory inspections without the stringent requirements that protect individuals' homes from searches. Regarding the Fifth

Amendment, protections against self-incrimination apply differently to corporations, particularly concerning business records, which cannot be shielded under self-incrimination claims. Some constitutional protections that are inherently personal, such as protection against degrading treatment or imprisonment, do not extend to corporations, which cannot experience physical punishment or incarceration. Corporations are therefore not equivalent to natural persons.

The *Citizens United* decision has intensified debate over whether corporations should possess the same political speech rights as individuals, particularly given the clear differences in rights, responsibilities, and consequences between corporate entities and human beings.

Truth About Corporate Taxes

Large, profitable corporations have been known to pay lower effective tax rates than individuals. Recent data highlights a significant advantage for major U.S. corporations following the Tax Cuts and Jobs Act (TCJA) of 2017. While individual taxpayers continue to face relatively stable effective tax burdens, the average effective tax rate for many large corporations declined from approximately 22 percent to about 12.8 percent, reflecting a shift in tax treatment favoring corporate entities.[257]

Multiple analyses, including reports from the Institute on Taxation and Economic Policy (ITEP), confirm this pattern. These studies show that many profitable corporations pay effective tax rates below 10 percent, with some paying between 0 and 5 percent. In contrast, middle-income individuals face an average effective tax rate of approximately 14 percent.[258,259]

Corporate Tax Trickle Down

The argument for maintaining low corporate tax rates is commonly referred to as supply-side or "trickle-down" economic theory. Proponents contend that lower corporate taxes allow businesses to reinvest profits into innovation, capital improvements, and workforce expansion, ultimately increasing wages and employment. However, many empirical analyses find that the primary beneficiaries of these tax reductions have been corporations and high-income individuals rather than average workers.

Studies, including research from the London School of Economics, show that decades of tax cuts for the wealthy have not produced meaningful gains in job growth or average incomes, while contributing to increased income inequality.[317] Research by economist Owen Zidar similarly found that tax cuts directed toward high-income groups had minimal effects on employment growth, whereas tax relief for lower-income households produced more substantial economic benefits.[318]

The Economic Policy Institute also reported that post-TCJA investment levels failed to support claims that corporate tax cuts significantly increased private investment.[319]

These findings indicate that a significant share of gains from such tax policies has been directed toward retained earnings, dividends, and executive compensation rather than broad-based wage growth or job creation.

Scaled Corporate Tax Rates

A graduated tax structure for corporations could address disparities in earning capacity while supporting entrepreneurship. Under such a system, larger and more profitable corporations would pay higher effective rates, while smaller businesses could receive relief or targeted incentives. Proponents argue that this approach would reduce competitive imbalances while ensuring sufficient revenue to fund government operations.

Businesses, individuals, and governments must also account for long-term inflation. An annual inflation rate of approximately 3 percent aligns with historical averages over the past 75 years and is often cited as consistent with stable economic growth.[59-31]

Thomas Jefferson addressed the importance of tax stability in a letter to J. W. Eppes in September 1813, writing, "The public contributions should be as uniform as practicable from year to year, that our habits of industry and of expense may become adapted to them; and that they may be duly digested and incorporated with our annual economy."[02] His observation underscores the value of predictable tax structures that allow individuals and businesses to plan prices, wages, and investment without continual disruption.

Taxation Today

Government operates on taxpayer revenue, and the broader economy depends on what individuals and businesses retain for spending and investment after taxes are collected. Expanding government requires greater extraction from the economy, while reducing government size and taxation leaves more capital in private circulation.

Stimulus payments function similarly to tax reductions by injecting money into the economy but remain infrequent and temporary. The United States began without an income tax, and Jefferson himself opposed income taxation, favoring consumption-based systems. A pure consumption tax could theoretically replace income taxes, but doing so would require a national sales or value-added tax rate exceeding 30 percent, along with safeguards to protect lower-income households.

A complete shift to a consumption-based system is not required to improve tax efficiency. More limited reforms, such as lowering income tax rates while broadening the tax base, may achieve many of the same goals with fewer unintended consequences. Because corporate tax burdens may be passed through to consumers, workers, or shareholders, changes to business taxation can affect prices, wages, and returns as well as revenues.

Any comprehensive restructuring of the tax system would therefore represent a major economic shift and must account for its effects on households, markets, and overall economic behavior.

Tax Rates

How the tax burden is distributed across income levels shapes incentives, economic behavior, and perceptions of fairness, making taxation central to both economic performance and system legitimacy.

Tax Burden and Distribution Across Income Levels

Tax systems allocate the cost of government across individuals and businesses. The structure of that allocation affects incentives, consumption, investment, and perceptions of fairness.

In 2020, individuals earning below $42,184 paid an average federal income tax rate of 3.1 percent, while the top 1 percent of earners paid an average rate of approximately 26 percent and accounted for 42.3 percent of total federal income taxes.[23-04] These figures reflect the progressive structure of the federal income tax system.

Income tax rates have remained relatively stable since the late twentieth century, but the distribution of tax burdens depends not only on statutory rates but also on deductions, credits, and the composition of income. Payroll taxes, consumption taxes, and indirect costs also affect the overall burden across income groups.

Debates over taxation often focus on whether systems are equitable, efficient, and supportive of economic growth. These objectives do not always align, requiring tradeoffs in policy design.

Jefferson on Taxation and Economic Balance

Debates over taxation have long reflected the tension between revenue needs and economic activity. In 1787, Thomas Jefferson wrote that "wealth acquired by speculation and plunder is fugacious in its nature and fills society with the spirit of gambling."[23-05]

Jefferson favored taxation that reflected capacity to pay and avoided undue burden in difficult periods. In a 1784 letter to James Madison, he suggested that taxes be tied to surplus production rather than gross output, so that individuals would contribute more in prosperous years and less in lean years.[23-06]

He also emphasized simplicity and predictability. In 1789, he wrote that taxes should be few and adjusted only as necessary to meet government needs.[23-07] Stability allows individuals and businesses to plan, while frequent or unpredictable changes can disrupt economic activity.

At the same time, Jefferson recognized practical constraints. Systems designed to be equitable may introduce variability in revenue. Balancing fairness, simplicity, and stability remains a central challenge in tax policy.

Taxation, Incentives, and Economic Activity

Taxation affects behavior by altering incentives. Higher tax rates reduce after tax returns on work and investment, while lower rates may encourage activity but reduce revenue.

Jefferson argued that excessive taxation can divert attention from productive activity, writing that taxation should not "attract the attention of our citizens from the pursuits of useful industry."[23-08] He later acknowledged that taxation is necessary for government function and cannot be eliminated entirely.

Public acceptance is a key factor. Jefferson noted that taxation is one of the functions of government most likely to encounter resistance, making alignment with public sentiment important for maintaining compliance and legitimacy.[23-09]

The effect of taxation on production depends on design. Predictable and transparent systems tend to have fewer distortions, while complex or uneven systems can alter behavior in unintended ways. At the same time, insufficient revenue can limit public investment in infrastructure, education, and security, which also affect economic performance.

Revenue, Expenditures, and Fiscal Balance

Government finances consist of revenues and expenditures. Primary sources of federal revenue include individual and corporate income taxes, payroll taxes for Social Security and Medicare, tariffs, and service fees.

In fiscal year 2024, total federal revenue was approximately $4.9 trillion. Individual income taxes generated about $2.2 trillion, and corporate income taxes approximately $420 billion.[23-10] The Internal Revenue Service processed more than 265 million returns and other forms, including roughly 160 million individual income tax returns.

Government expenditures include operating costs, defense, entitlement programs such as Social Security and Medicare, and other domestic and international obligations. In fiscal year 2024, federal spending reached approximately

$6.75 trillion, exceeding revenues and resulting in a deficit of about $1.9 trillion.[23-11]

Fiscal balance depends on both revenue and spending decisions. Persistent deficits increase public debt, affecting interest costs and future policy flexibility.

Tariffs, Trade, and Indirect Taxation

Tariffs are taxes on imported goods and serve both revenue and policy functions, protecting domestic industries, addressing trade imbalances, and responding to foreign subsidies or dumping practices.

Tariffs can affect prices by increasing the cost of imported goods and inputs. Evidence from recent trade actions indicates that tariffs are often passed through to domestic prices, raising costs for consumers and businesses.[23-12]

Debate over trade policy reflects differing priorities. Supporters emphasize domestic industry protection and national security. Critics highlight higher consumer prices, reduced efficiency, and the potential for retaliatory measures.

Tariffs can also interact with environmental and regulatory differences across countries. Policies that adjust tariffs based on production standards may address these differences but can increase complexity and costs.

As a source of revenue, tariffs represent a smaller share of total federal income than direct taxes. Their primary impact is indirect, affecting prices, production, and trade relationships.

Complexity, Simplification, and Policy Design

Tax systems often become complex over time as exemptions, deductions, and credits are added to achieve policy goals. These provisions can encourage behaviors such as homeownership, education, or investment, but they also increase administrative burden and reduce transparency.

Simplification is frequently proposed as a reform objective. A simpler system can reduce compliance costs and improve understanding, but it may also remove incentives embedded in existing provisions.

Design choices involve tradeoffs. Eliminating deductions may broaden the tax base and lower rates, but it can also change incentives and distributional outcomes. The challenge is to balance clarity, efficiency, and policy objectives.

Behavioral Taxes and Targeted Incentives

Governments often use taxes to influence behavior. Deductions, credits, and excise taxes are applied to encourage or discourage specific activities.

Excise taxes apply to particular goods or services, often those associated with public health concerns. These taxes can reduce consumption and generate revenue for related programs, but are often regressive and affect lower-income households more heavily.

Excise taxes have declined as a share of federal revenue over time, accounting for a small percentage of total receipts.[23-13] Their impact is therefore targeted rather than systemic, affecting specific sectors rather than overall revenue.

Behavioral taxation raises questions about effectiveness and equity. While such taxes can influence behavior, they can also create unintended consequences, including shifts to informal markets or substitution effects.

Taxation, Legitimacy, and System Stability

Taxation is not only an economic mechanism but also a source of political legitimacy. Systems that are perceived as fair and predictable are more likely to maintain compliance and support.

Perceptions of fairness depend on both distribution and transparency. When taxpayers understand how burdens are allocated and how revenues are used, trust may increase. When systems are perceived as complex or uneven, trust may decline.

Tax policy interacts with broader economic outcomes. Decisions about taxation influence income distribution, investment, and public services. These effects shape both economic performance and social stability.

Because taxation reflects choices about distribution and responsibility, it connects directly to broader questions of governance. The design of tax systems influences not only revenue, but how economic gains and obligations are shared across society.

Closing

Systems, Incentives, and Choice

Economic, social, and political outcomes are not independent, resulting from system design, incentives, and the distribution of power. Throughout this work, a consistent pattern emerges. Policy sets incentives, Incentives direct capital allocation, capital allocation influences business decisions, and business decisions determine jobs, income, and stability. Those outcomes shape social conditions, institutional trust, and political pressure, which in turn feeds back into policy. This is not a theory. It is a system.

Structure Drives Outcomes

Outcomes that are often treated as separate problems are connected through shared incentives and capital flows. Wage stagnation, inequality, declining trust, workforce instability, and political polarization do not arise independently but result from how incentives operate within the system.

When policy and market conditions favor capital over labor, a larger share of income flows to ownership rather than wages. When institutions shift risk to individuals, income becomes less stable and exposure to loss increases. When information is uneven, those with better data or access gain pricing and decision power. When opportunity narrows, trust in institutions declines.

These outcomes are shaped by how incentives, risk, and information are structured, not isolated events. Recognizing these connections shifts the focus from symptoms to underlying causes.

Technology and System Acceleration

Technological change works through existing systems and amplifies their effects. Automation increases productivity but can reduce the demand for labor in specific tasks. Artificial intelligence expands decision-making capacity while concentrating control in those who own data and infrastructure. Robotics extends digital systems into the physical world, altering how work is performed and how production is organized.

These changes interact with existing incentives. If productivity gains are broadly distributed, technology can improve living standards. If gains concentrate in ownership and control, disparities can widen. The outcome depends less on the technology itself than on how systems allocate its benefits.

Technology increases the speed and scale of change, but the need for governance remains.

Risk, Responsibility, and Adaptation

A central shift in modern economic systems is the movement of risk. Traditional employment structures absorbed many uncertainties through stable wages, benefits, and institutional protections. As work becomes more fragmented, risk increasingly shifts to individuals, making income less predictable, benefits less certain, and transitions more frequent.

Adaptation is often framed as an individual responsibility. Workers are expected to retrain, relocate, and adjust to changing conditions, but these expectations assume access to time, resources, and opportunity that are not evenly distributed. Whether risk is borne primarily by individuals or shared across institutions is not determined by technology. It is a choice embedded in policy, market design, and social systems.

Measurement and Perception

What is measured influences what is valued. Traditional indicators such as gross domestic product and employment rates capture output and participation, but they do not fully reflect stability, opportunity, or long-term well-being. An economy can grow while large segments of the population experience stagnation or insecurity.

When measurement focuses on output alone, systems may reward efficiency without accounting for distribution or resilience. Expanding how outcomes are measured can provide a more complete view of economic performance, but it also introduces complexity and tradeoffs. Measurement influences how outcomes are evaluated and acted upon, even though results are driven by underlying conditions.

Trust and Legitimacy

Economic systems depend on trust as well as performance. Consumers must trust that products are safe and contracts are fair. Workers must believe that effort can lead to improvement. Citizens must have confidence that institutions operate within clear and enforceable rules.

When outcomes diverge from expectations, trust declines. When systems appear opaque or unresponsive, legitimacy weakens. Maintaining trust requires transparency, accountability, and consistent application of rules, not just efficiency.

Governance and Tradeoffs

Markets allocate resources, and governments establish rules. Neither operates independently. Decisions about taxation, regulation, education, labor, and trade define the boundaries within which markets function and determine how incentives are structured and how outcomes are distributed.

Governance manages tradeoffs rather than eliminating them. Policies that increase efficiency may affect distribution. Policies that increase stability may affect incentives. Policies that expand access may require additional resources. These tradeoffs are unavoidable, and effective governance requires making them explicit rather than obscuring them.

Choice and Responsibility

Economic outcomes are often treated as automatic, as if technology or markets produce results on their own. They do not. Outcomes depend on how rules are written, how incentives are set, and who carries the risk. Those choices are not fixed. Decisions about taxation, regulation, work organization, and ownership determine how income is distributed, how stable work is, and who benefits from growth.

No system can maximize everything at once. Policies that favor efficiency can increase concentration. Policies that increase stability can reduce flexibility. Policies that expand access can require higher costs. These are tradeoffs, not errors.

Disagreement reflects priorities, not misunderstanding.

Adaptation and System Capacity

There is no single model that defines a successful system. Conditions change, technologies evolve, and societies differ in their priorities. A durable system requires the capacity to adapt without losing legitimacy.

That capacity depends on clear rules, transparent processes, and institutions that can adjust to changing conditions. It also depends on an informed public capable of evaluating tradeoffs. Stability comes from managing change within a system that remains credible.

System Awareness

Understanding how systems operate provides a framework for evaluating outcomes. When issues are viewed in isolation, responses tend to be fragmented. When connections are recognized, it becomes possible to address underlying causes rather than symptoms.

Policy, incentives, capital, work, and outcomes are part of a continuous system. Changes in one part affect the others. Awareness of these relationships allows for more deliberate decisions and more consistent results.

Closing Comments

Over the next 250 years, technological change will continue. Markets will continue to evolve. Economic conditions will continue to shift. The central issue is not change itself, but how that change is governed.

Systems shape outcomes, incentives guide behavior, and power influences both. Understanding that relationship provides a basis for making informed and accountable choices.

ALSO BY CHARLES PATTON

- **Our Next 250 Years –** Representation and Influence
  First Companion work to this book
- **Our Next 250 Years -** Power and Control
  Second Companion work to this book
- **Mastering Strategy**
  The essential guide to thinking, planning, and winning in any field.
- **Extreme Leadership**
  Decision-making and accountability under pressure
- **In Defense of the Righteous**
  A gripping story of moral courage when justice and survival collide.
- **Tigers of the Ice**
  Adventure meets survival in an unforgiving world where instinct rules.
- **Thinking**
  Learn how to think more clearly, act decisively, and change your life.
- **Artificial Consciousness**
  Explores the frontier of automating consciousness.
- **The Gardener's Secret and Other Stories**
  Mysteries and dramas revealing the hidden motives behind ordinary lives.
- **Who Do You Trust**
  A deadly game of deceit between two spies and one truth.
- **Busted, What's Wrong With My Excuse**
  An entertaining look at excuses people make, and how to excuse better.
- **Naked Reflections**
  Raw, honest poetry of truth, ego, and the search for authenticity.
- **Charles Patton, Visionaire**
  Insights from a lifetime of ideas, invention, and fearless creativity.
- **Storming the Castle Bridge**
  A tale of rebellion, loyalty, and the unbreakable human will to be free.

Find every title at: charlespattonbooks.com

APPENDICES

Copy and paste the following links for the details of:

The Constitution of the United States
https://charlespattonbooks.com/Constitution.php

The Declaration of the Rights of Man – 1789
https://charlespattonbooks.com/RightsofMan.php

The U.N.'s Declaration of Human Rights
https://charlespattonbooks.com/HumanRights.php

REFERENCES

01-06. Congressional Budget Office. *The Budget and Economic Outlook: 2024 to 2034*. U.S. Government Publishing Office, 2024.

01-07. Internal Revenue Service. *SOI Tax Stats – Number of Pages in the Internal Revenue Code and Regulations*. U.S. Department of the Treasury, 2023.

01-08. Office of the Federal Register. *Federal Register Document Pages Published Annually*. National Archives, 2023.

01-09. Office of the Federal Register. *Code of Federal Regulations (CFR) Total Page Count*. National Archives, 2023.

01-10. Office of Management and Budget. *United States Government Manual*. U.S. Government Publishing Office, 2023.

01-11. Bureau of Economic Analysis. *Gross Domestic Product, Fourth Quarter and Year 2023 (Advance Estimate)*. U.S. Department of Commerce, 2024.

01-12. Federal Reserve Board. *Monetary Policy Report*. Board of Governors of the Federal Reserve System, 2024.

01-13. Autor, David, et al. "The Fall of the Labor Share and the Rise of Superstar Firms." *Quarterly Journal of Economics*, vol. 135, no. 2, 2020, pp. 645–709.

01-14. De Loecker, Jan, et al. "The Rise of Market Power and the Macroeconomic Implications." *Quarterly Journal of Economics*, vol. 135, no. 2, 2020, pp. 561–644.

01-15. Board of Governors of the Federal Reserve System. *Monetary Policy Report*. 2021–2024.

02-01. McKinsey Global Institute. *Global Financial Markets: Structure and Scale*. McKinsey & Company, 2023.

02-02. United Nations Conference on Trade and Development. *World Investment Report 2023*. United Nations, 2023.

02-03. International Federation of Robotics. *World Robotics Report 2023*. IFR, 2023.

02-04. Federal Reserve Bank of New York. "Corporate Share Repurchases." 2023.

03-01. Bureau of Labor Statistics. *Contingent and Alternative Employment Arrangements*. U.S. Department of Labor, 2023.

03-02. Economic Policy Institute. *CEO Pay Has Skyrocketed 1978–2022*. EPI, 2023.

03-03. Federal Reserve Bank of St. Louis. *Corporate Profits and Capital Expenditures Data*. FRED Database, 2024.

03-04. Bureau of Labor Statistics. *Labor Productivity and Costs*. U.S. Department of Labor, 2024.

04-01. Bureau of Labor Statistics. *Employment, Hours, and Earnings from the Current Employment Statistics Survey*. U.S. Department of Labor, 2024.

04-03. Bureau of Labor Statistics. *Union Members — 1983 to 2023 Historical Tables*. U.S. Department of Labor, 2024.

04-04. Bureau of Labor Statistics. *Employee Tenure in 2022*. U.S. Department of Labor, 2023.

04-05. Bureau of Labor Statistics. *Job Openings and Labor Turnover Survey (JOLTS)*. U.S. Department of Labor, 2024.

04-07. Congressional Budget Office. *The Distribution of Household Income, 1979 to 2019*. Congressional Budget Office, 2023.

04-08. Pew Research Center. "For Most U.S. Workers, Real Wages Have Barely Budged for Decades." *Pew Research Center*, 7 Aug. 2018, https://www.pewresearch.org/social-trends/2018/08/07/for-most-u-s-workers-real-wages-have-barely-budged-for-decades/.

04-09. World Inequality Database. "United States: Income Inequality." *World Inequality Database*, https://wid.world/country/usa/.

05-01. Bureau of Labor Statistics. *Employment and Earnings Data*. U.S. Department of Labor, 2024.

05-02. Bureau of Labor Statistics. *Employer Costs for Employee Compensation*. U.S. Department of Labor, 2024.

05-03. Federal Reserve Board. *Distribution of Household Wealth in the United States*. Board of Governors of the Federal Reserve System, 2024.

05-04. Bureau of Labor Statistics. *Employer Costs for Employee Compensation*. U.S. Department of Labor, 2025.

05-05. Employee Benefit Research Institute. *Employee Benefits in Total Compensation*. EBRI, 2014.

05-06. Bureau of Labor Statistics. *ERISA at 50: BLS Tracks the Evolution of Retirement Benefits*. U.S. Department of Labor, 2024.

05-07. Bureau of Labor Statistics. *National Compensation Survey: Employee Benefits in the United States*. U.S. Department of Labor, 2023.

06-01. Bureau of Economic Analysis. *Gross Domestic Product, 2024*. U.S. Department of Commerce, 2025.

06-02. Congressional Budget Office. *The Budget and Economic Outlook: 2024 to 2034*. U.S. Government Publishing Office, 2024.

06-04. Bureau of Labor Statistics. *The Employment Situation — Historical Data*. U.S. Department of Labor, 2024.

06-05. Bureau of Labor Statistics. *Labor Force Statistics from the Current Population Survey*. U.S. Department of Labor, 2024.

06-06. Chetty, Raj, et al. *The Fading American Dream: Trends in Absolute Income Mobility since 1940*. National Bureau of Economic Research, 2017.

06-07. Chetty, Raj, et al. "The Equality of Opportunity Project." Harvard University, https://opportunityinsights.org/

07-01. Bureau of Economic Analysis. "Gross Domestic Product, 4th Quarter and Year 2024 (Advance Estimate)." U.S. Department of Commerce, 25 Jan. 2025.

07-02. World Bank. "Trade (% of GDP), United States." World Development Indicators, 2024.

07-03. Federal Reserve Board. "Global Supply Chain Disruptions and U.S. Economic Activity." Board of Governors of the Federal Reserve System, 2022.

07-04. U.S. International Trade Commission. "Global Value Chains and U.S. Manufacturing." USITC, 2023.

07-05. U.S. Geological Survey. Mineral Commodity Summaries 2025. U.S. Department of the Interior, 2025.

07-06. Semiconductor Industry Association. "2024 State of the U.S. Semiconductor Industry." SIA, 2024.

07-07. U.S. Energy Information Administration. "Short-Term Energy Outlook." U.S. Department of Energy, 2024.

07-08. U.S. Department of Commerce. "CHIPS and Science Act Fact Sheet." 2023.

07-09. U.S. Department of the Treasury. "Inflation Reduction Act Guidebook." 2023.

07-10. Office of Management and Budget. *Historical Tables, Budget of the U.S. Government, Fiscal Year 2025*. Table 2.1, "Receipts by Source: 1934–2029." Executive Office of the President, 2024.

07-11. Congressional Budget Office. *The Budget and Economic Outlook: 2024 to 2034*. Congressional Budget Office, 2024.

07-12. Internal Revenue Service. *Statistics of Income: Individual Income Tax Returns, 2021*. Internal Revenue Service, U.S. Department of the Treasury, 2024.

07-14. Powell, Lisa M., et al. "A Systematic Review of the Impact of Sugar-Sweetened Beverage Taxes on Purchases and Consumption." *American Journal of Clinical Nutrition*, vol. 105, no. 3, 2017, pp. 735–746.

07-15. Congressional Budget Office. *The Budget and Economic Outlook: 2024 to 2034*. Congressional Budget Office, 2024.

07-16. U.S. Department of Agriculture, Economic Research Service. *Farm Household Income and Characteristics*. U.S. Department of Agriculture, 2024.

08-01. Office of Management and Budget. *Historical Tables, Budget of the U.S. Government, Fiscal Year 2025*. Table 1.1, "Summary of Receipts, Outlays, and Surpluses or Deficits: 1789–2029." Executive Office of the President, 2024.

08-02. Board of Governors of the Federal Reserve System. *The Federal Reserve System: Purposes and Functions*. 11th ed., Federal Reserve, 2023.

08-03. Board of Governors of the Federal Reserve System. "Federal Funds Effective Rate." *FRED, Federal Reserve Bank of St. Louis*, 2024.

08-04. Federal Reserve Bank of St. Louis. "30-Year Fixed Rate Mortgage Average in the United States." *FRED, Federal Reserve Bank of St. Louis*, 2024.

08-05. Congressional Budget Office. *The Budget and Economic Outlook: 2024 to 2034*. Congressional Budget Office, 2024.

08-06. Bureau of Labor Statistics. "Consumer Price Index for All Urban Consumers (CPI-U)." U.S. Department of Labor, 2024.

09-01. Board of Governors of the Federal Reserve System. "M2 Money Stock (M2SL)." *FRED, Federal Reserve Bank of St. Louis*, 2024.

09-02. Board of Governors of the Federal Reserve System. *The Federal Reserve System: Purposes and Functions*. 11th ed., Federal Reserve, 2023.

09-03. Bureau of Labor Statistics. "Consumer Price Index for All Urban Consumers (CPI-U): All Items." U.S. Department of Labor, 2024.

09-04. Board of Governors of the Federal Reserve System. "Federal Funds Effective Rate." *FRED, Federal Reserve Bank of St. Louis*, 2024.

09-05. Office of the Federal Register. *Code of Federal Regulations (CFR) Annual Edition*. National Archives and Records Administration, 2024.

09-06. Office of Information and Regulatory Affairs. *Regulatory Plan and Unified Agenda of Federal Regulatory and Deregulatory Actions*. Office of Management and Budget, 2024.

09-07. Crain, W. Mark, and Nicole V. Crain. *The Cost of Federal Regulation to the U.S. Economy, Manufacturing, and Small Business*. National Association of Manufacturers, 2014.

09-08. National Federation of Independent Business. *Small Business Problems and Priorities*. NFIB Research Foundation, 2020.

09-09. Board of Governors of the Federal Reserve System. *Federal Reserve Actions to Support the Flow of Credit to Households and Businesses*. Federal Reserve, 2020.

09-10. U.S. Securities and Exchange Commission. *SEC Enforcement Results: Fiscal Year 2023*. U.S. Securities and Exchange Commission, 2023.

09-11. West Virginia v. Environmental Protection Agency, 597 U.S. 697. Supreme Court of the United States, 2022.

09-12. Chevron U.S.A. Inc. v. Natural Resources Defense Council, 467 U.S. 837. Supreme Court of the United States, 1984.

09-13. West Virginia v. Environmental Protection Agency, 597 U.S. 697. Supreme Court of the United States, 2022.

10-03. Infrastructure Investment and Jobs Act, Pub. L. No. 117-58, 135 Stat. 429 (2021).

10-04. Congressional Budget Office. *The Budgetary Effects of Laws Enacted in Response to the 2020–2021 Coronavirus Pandemic*. Congressional Budget Office, 2022.

10-05. Congressional Budget Office. *The 2024 Long-Term Budget Outlook*. Congressional Budget Office, 2024.

10-06. Congressional Budget Office. *Monthly Budget Review: Summary for Fiscal Year 2024*. Congressional Budget Office, 2024.

10-07. Social Security Administration. *The 2024 Annual Report of the Board of Trustees of the Federal Old-Age and Survivors Insurance and Federal Disability Insurance Trust Funds*. Social Security Administration, 2024.

11-01. U.S. Bureau of Economic Analysis, *National Income and Product Accounts Tables*, Table 5.3.5 "Gross Private Domestic Investment as a Percent of Gross Domestic Product" and Table 1.1.5 "Gross Domestic Product," Bureau of Economic Analysis, U.S. Department of Commerce, 2020–2024.

11-02. U.S. Bureau of Economic Analysis, *National Income and Product Accounts Tables*, Table 6.16D "Corporate Profits After Tax (without Inventory Valuation Adjustment and Capital Consumption Adjustment)," Bureau of Economic Analysis, U.S. Department of Commerce, 2022–2024.

11-03. U.S. Bureau of Economic Analysis, *Direct Investment Position in the United States on a Historical-Cost Basis, Country and Industry Detail*, Bureau of Economic Analysis, U.S. Department of Commerce, 2023.

11-04. Securities Industry and Financial Markets Association (SIFMA), *US Corporate Bond Market Statistics: Issuance and Outstanding*, SIFMA Research, 2023.

11-05. U.S. Small Business Administration, Office of Advocacy, *Small Business GDP: Update 2002–2022* and *Frequently Asked Questions About Small Business 2023*, U.S. Small Business Administration, 2023.

11-06. Federal Reserve Banks, *2023 Small Business Credit Survey: Report on Employer Firms*, Federal Reserve System, 2023.

11-07. Federal Reserve Bank of New York, *Corporate Bond Market Distress and Issuance Trends During the COVID-19 Pandemic*, Federal Reserve Bank of New York, 2020.

11-08. Board of Governors of the Federal Reserve System, *Report on the Economic Well-Being of U.S. Households in 2023* and *Small Business Credit Conditions*, Federal Reserve System, 2023.

11-09. Board of Governors of the Federal Reserve System, *Financial Accounts of the United States, Z.1 Statistical Release*, Federal Reserve System, 2024.

11-10. McKinsey & Company, *Global Private Markets Review 2023: Private Markets Turn Down the Volume*, McKinsey Global Institute, 2023.

11-11. National Venture Capital Association and PitchBook, *Venture Monitor: US Venture Capital Activity Full-Year 2021*, NVCA and PitchBook, 2022.

11-12. Autor, David, Dorn, David, Katz, Lawrence F., Patterson, Christina, and Van Reenen, John, "The Fall of the Labor Share and the Rise of Superstar Firms," *American Economic Review*, Vol. 110, No. 3, March 2020, pp. 645–709.

11-13. U.S. Census Bureau, *Economic Census: Concentration Ratios (CR4 and CR8) by Industry*, U.S. Census Bureau, 2017–2022.

11-14. Board of Governors of the Federal Reserve System, *Distribution of Corporate Assets and Revenues by Firm Size, Financial Accounts Supplementary Tables*, Federal Reserve System, 2023.

11-15. National Venture Capital Association and PitchBook, *Geographic Distribution of Venture Capital Investment*, Venture Monitor Report, NVCA and PitchBook, 2023.

11-16. U.S. Small Business Administration, *7(a) Loan Program Performance Report and Annual Lending Statistics*, U.S. Small Business Administration, 2023.

12-01. U.S. Bureau of Economic Analysis, *U.S. Direct Investment Abroad: Balance of Payments and Direct Investment Position Data*, Bureau of Economic Analysis, U.S. Department of Commerce, 2023.

12-02. U.S. Bureau of Economic Analysis, *Foreign Direct Investment in the United States: Balance of Payments and Direct Investment Position Data*, Bureau of Economic Analysis, U.S. Department of Commerce, 2023.

12-03. Institute of International Finance, *Global Capital Flows Report: Emerging Markets Portfolio Flows and Debt Trends*, Institute of International Finance, 2022.

12-04. McKinsey Global Institute, *The Rise and Rise of the Global Balance Sheet: How Productively Are We Using Our Wealth?*, McKinsey Global Institute, 2021.

13. " UNAFEI. August 2023.
http://www.unafei.or.jp/english/pdf/PDF_rms/no56/56-12.pdf.

13-01. U.S. Census Bureau, *Economic Census: Concentration Ratios (CR4 and CR8) by Industry*, U.S. Census Bureau, 2017–2022.

13-02. Autor, David, Dorn, David, Katz, Lawrence F., Patterson, Christina, and Van Reenen, John, "The Fall of the Labor Share and the Rise of Superstar Firms," American Economic Review, Vol. 110, No. 3, March 2020, pp. 645–709.

13-03. De Loecker, Jan, Eeckhout, Jan, and Unger, Gabriel, "The Rise of Market Power and the Macroeconomic Implications," Quarterly Journal of Economics, Vol. 135, No. 2, May 2020, pp. 561–644.

13-04. Institute for Mergers, Acquisitions and Alliances (IMAA), *M&A Statistics Worldwide: Number and Value of Deals*, 2023.

13-05. Azar, José, Marinescu, Ioana, and Steinbaum, Marshall, "Labor Market Concentration," Journal of Human Resources, Vol. 57, No. S, 2022, pp. S167–S199.

14-01. U.S. Census Bureau, *Economic Census: Concentration Ratios (CR4 and CR8) by Industry*, U.S. Census Bureau, 2017–2022.

14-02. Autor, David, Dorn, David, Katz, Lawrence F., Patterson, Christina, and Van Reenen, John, "The Fall of the Labor Share and the Rise of Superstar Firms," *American Economic Review*, Vol. 110, No. 3, March 2020, pp. 645–709.

14-03. De Loecker, Jan, Eeckhout, Jan, and Unger, Gabriel, "The Rise of Market Power and the Macroeconomic Implications," *Quarterly Journal of Economics*, Vol. 135, No. 2, May 2020, pp. 561–644.

14-04. Grullon, Gustavo, Larkin, Yelena, and Michaely, Roni, "Are U.S. Industries Becoming More Concentrated?" *Review of Finance*, Vol. 23, No. 4, July 2019, pp. 697–743.

14-05. Azar, José, Marinescu, Ioana, and Steinbaum, Marshall, "Labor Market Concentration," *Journal of Human Resources*, Vol. 57, No. S, 2022, pp. S167–S199.

14-06. U.S. Department of Justice and Federal Trade Commission, *Horizontal Merger Guidelines*, U.S. Department of Justice and Federal Trade Commission, 2010 (updated 2023 draft guidelines).

14-07. Federal Trade Commission, *Annual Report to Congress on Antitrust Enforcement*, Federal Trade Commission, 2023.

14-08. European Commission, *Regulation (EU) 2022/1925 on Contestable and Fair Markets in the Digital Sector (Digital Markets Act)*, Official Journal of the European Union, 2022.

14-10. U.S. Patent and Trademark Office, *Performance and Accountability Report*, U.S. Department of Commerce, 2023.

14-11. Congressional Research Service, *Antitrust Law: An Introduction*, Congressional Research Service Report R45831, updated 2023.

14-12. Institute for Mergers, Acquisitions and Alliances, *M&A Statistics Worldwide: Number and Value of Deals*, IMAA Institute, 2023.

14-13. McKinsey Global Institute, *The Rise and Rise of the Global Balance Sheet: How Productively Are We Using Our Wealth?*, McKinsey Global Institute, 2021.

14-15. Lancieri, Filippo, Posner, Eric A., and Zingales, Luigi, "The Political Economy of the Decline of Antitrust Enforcement in the United States," SSRN Working Paper, revised 2023.

14-16. Federal Trade Commission and U.S. Department of Justice, *Hart-Scott-Rodino Annual Report*, Fiscal Year 2024, Federal Trade Commission, 2025.

14-17. Covington & Burling LLP, *Merger Enforcement Activity Continues at Historically Low Levels*, Antitrust Client Advisory, 2024.

14-20, Reich, Robert B. *The System: Who Rigged It, How We Fix It*. New York, Alfred A. Knopf, 2020.

15-01. Fichtner, Jan, Heemskerk, Eelke M., and Garcia-Bernardo, Javier, "Hidden Power of the Big Three? Passive Index Funds, Re-Concentration of Corporate Ownership, and New Financial Risk," *Business and Politics*, Vol. 19, No. 2, June 2017, pp. 298–326.

15-02. Federal Reserve Board, *Financial Accounts of the United States, Distributional Financial Accounts*, Board of Governors of the Federal Reserve System, 2023.

15-03. La Porta, Rafael, Lopez-de-Silanes, Florencio, and Shleifer, Andrei, "Corporate Ownership Around the World," *Journal of Finance*, Vol. 54, No. 2, April 1999, pp. 471–517.

15-04. McKinsey & Company, *Global Private Markets Review 2023: Private Markets Turn Down the Volume*, McKinsey Global Institute, 2023.

15-05. Federal Reserve Board, *Financial Accounts of the United States, Corporate Equities by Sector and Holder*, Board of Governors of the Federal Reserve System, 2023.

15-06. Federal Reserve Board, *Financial Accounts of the United States, Nonfinancial Corporate Business; Debt Securities and Loans Outstanding*, Board of Governors of the Federal Reserve System, 2024.

15-07. Council of Institutional Investors, *Dual-Class IPO Statistics and Trends*, Council of Institutional Investors, 2023.

16-01. U.S. Congress, *CHIPS and Science Act of 2022*, Public Law 117–167, 117th Congress, August 9, 2022.
U.S. Department of Commerce, *CHIPS for America Program Overview*, National Institute of Standards and Technology, 2023. https://www.nist.gov/chips Accessed February 27, 2026.

16-02. U.S. Customs and Border Protection, *U.S. Border Patrol Nationwide Apprehensions and Border Security Metrics*, U.S. Department of Homeland Security, 2023.
U.S. Customs and Border Protection, *Border Security Overview and U.S. Border Length Data*, 2023.
https://www.cbp.gov/newsroom/stats. Accessed February 27, 2026.

16-03. Board of Governors of the Federal Reserve System, *Financial Accounts of the United States (Z.1), Household Net Worth Levels*, Table B.101, 2010. Federal Reserve Bank of St. Louis (FRED), *Households; Net Worth, Level (HNONWPD)*, 2007–

2009. https://fred.stlouisfed.org/series/HNONWPD. Accessed February 27, 2026.

16-04. U.S. Bureau of Labor Statistics, *Consumer Price Index Summary, June 2022*, U.S. Department of Labor, July 13, 2022. https://www.bls.gov/news.release/cpi.nr0.htm. Accessed February 27, 2026.

16-05. World Bank, *World Development Indicators: Trade (% of GDP)*, World Bank Group, 2023. https://data.worldbank.org/indicator/NE.TRD.GNFS.ZS. Accessed February 27, 2026.

16-06. U.S. Bureau of Labor Statistics, *All Employees, Manufacturing (CES3000000001)*, Current Employment Statistics, U.S. Department of Labor, 2024. Federal Reserve Bank of St. Louis (FRED), *Manufacturing Employment Series*, 2000–2024. https://fred.stlouisfed.org/series/CES3000000001 Accessed February 27, 2026.

16-07. Board of Governors of the Federal Reserve System, *Federal Funds Effective Rate*, Statistical Release H.15, 2024. Federal Reserve Bank of St. Louis (FRED), *Federal Funds Effective Rate (FEDFUNDS)*, 2022–2024. https://fred.stlouisfed.org/series/FEDFUNDS. Accessed February 27, 2026.

17-01. Greenwood, Robin, and Scharfstein, David, "The Growth of Finance," Journal of Economic Perspectives, Vol. 27, No. 2, Spring 2013, pp. 3–28. https://www.aeaweb.org/articles?id=10.1257/jep.27.2.3 Accessed February 27, 2026.

17-02. Philippon, Thomas, "Finance vs. Wal-Mart: Why Are Financial Services So Expensive?" American Economic Review, Vol. 105, No. 5, May 2015, pp. 140–144. https://www.aeaweb.org/articles?id=10.1257/aer.p20151052 Accessed February 27, 2026.

17-03. S&P Dow Jones Indices, S&P 500 Buybacks Quarterly Report, 2024.

https://www.spglobal.com/spdji/en/documents/additional-material/sp-500-buybacks.pdf Accessed February 27, 2026.

17-04. Board of Governors of the Federal Reserve System, Financial Accounts of the United States, Nonfinancial Corporate Business; Debt Securities and Loans Outstanding, Table L.102, 2024. https://www.federalreserve.gov/releases/z1/ Accessed February 27, 2026.

17-05. McKinsey & Company, Global Private Markets Review 2023: Private Markets Turn Down the Volume, McKinsey Global Institute, 2023. https://www.mckinsey.com/industries/private-capital/our-insights/global-private-markets-review Accessed February 27, 2026.

18-01. U.S. Bureau of Labor Statistics, *Consumer Expenditure Survey, Income and Earnings Data*, U.S. Department of Labor, 2024. https://www.bls.gov/cex/ Accessed February 27, 2026.

18-02. Paul, Karsten I., and Moser, Klaus, "Unemployment Impairs Mental Health: Meta-Analyses," *Journal of Vocational Behavior*, Vol. 74, No. 3, June 2009, pp. 264–282. https://doi.org/10.1016/j.jvb.2009.01.001 Accessed February 27, 2026.

18-03. U.S. Bureau of Labor Statistics, *Employment by Major Industry Sector*, Current Employment Statistics, U.S. Department of Labor, 2024. https://www.bls.gov/emp/tables/employment-by-major-industry-sector.htm Accessed February 27, 2026.

18-04. Katz, Lawrence F., and Krueger, Alan B., "The Rise and Nature of Alternative Work Arrangements in the United States, 1995–2015," *National Bureau of Economic Research Working Paper No. 22667*, 2016. https://www.nber.org/papers/w22667 Accessed February 27, 2026

.

18-05. Case, Anne, and Deaton, Angus, "Mortality and Morbidity in the 21st Century," *Brookings Papers on Economic Activity*, Spring 2017, pp. 397–476. https://www.brookings.edu/bpea-articles/mortality-and-morbidity-in-the-21st-century/ Accessed February 27, 2026.

18-06. U.S. Bureau of Labor Statistics, *Employee Benefits in the United States, March 2024*, U.S. Department of Labor, 2024. https://www.bls.gov/news.release/ebs2.nr0.htm Accessed February 27, 2026.

18-07. U.S. Bureau of Labor Statistics, *Labor Force Statistics from the Current Population Survey, Part-Time Employment*, U.S. Department of Labor, 2024. https://www.bls.gov/cps Accessed February 27, 2026.

18-08. U.S. Bureau of Labor Statistics, *Self-Employment Data from the Current Population Survey*, U.S. Department of Labor, 2024. https://www.bls.gov/cps Accessed February 27, 2026.

18-09. U.S. Bureau of Labor Statistics, *Employee Tenure Summary*, U.S. Department of Labor, 2024. https://www.bls.gov/news.release/tenure.nr0.htm Accessed February 27, 2026.

18-10. U.S. Bureau of Labor Statistics, *National Compensation Survey: Retirement Benefits*, U.S. Department of Labor, 2024. https://www.bls.gov/ncs Accessed February 27, 2026.

18-11. McKinsey Global Institute, *A Future That Works: Automation, Employment, and Productivity*, McKinsey & Company, January 2017. https://www.mckinsey.com/featured-insights/future-of-work Accessed February 27, 2026.

18-12. U.S. Bureau of Labor Statistics, *American Time Use Survey and Remote Work Estimates*, U.S. Department of Labor, 2024. https://www.bls.gov/atus Accessed February 27, 2026.

18-13. McKinsey Global Institute, *Generative AI and the Future of Work in America*, McKinsey & Company, 2023. https://www.mckinsey.com/featured-insights/future-of-work/generative-ai-and-the-future-of-work-in-america Accessed February 27, 2026.

18-14. Economic Policy Institute, *The Productivity–Pay Gap*, Economic Policy Institute, 2023. https://www.epi.org/productivity-pay-gap/ Accessed February 27, 2026.

18-15. Board of Governors of the Federal Reserve System, *Distribution of Household Wealth in the United States since 1989*, Distributional Financial Accounts, 2024. https://www.federalreserve.gov/releases/z1/dataviz/dfa/distribute/table/ Accessed February 27, 2026.

18-16. Federal Reserve Bank of New York, *Quarterly Report on Household Debt and Credit*, Federal Reserve Bank of New York, 2024. https://www.newyorkfed.org/microeconomics/hhdc Accessed February 27, 2026.

19-05. U.S. Chamber of Commerce. *Understanding America's Labor Shortage: The Most Impacted Industries*. U.S. Chamber of Commerce, 2023, https://www.uschamber.com/workforce/understanding-americas-labor-shortage.

19-06. World Economic Forum. *The Future of Jobs Report 2023*. World Economic Forum, 2023, https://www.weforum.org/reports/the-future-of-jobs-report-2023/.

19-08. Federal Reserve Bank of New York. *Quarterly Report on Household Debt and Credit*. Federal Reserve Bank of New York, 2024, https://www.newyorkfed.org/microeconomics/hhdc.html.

19-09. Board of Governors of the Federal Reserve System. *Report on the Economic Well-Being of U.S. Households in 2023*. Federal Reserve, 2024, https://www.federalreserve.gov/publications/economic-well-being-of-us-households.htm.

19-10. U.S. Department of Education, Federal Student Aid. *Portfolio by Debt Size*. Federal Student Aid Data Center, 2024, https://studentaid.gov/data-center/student/portfolio.

19-11. Looney, Adam, and Constantine Yannelis. "A Crisis in Student Loans? How Changes in the Characteristics of Borrowers and in the Institutions They Attended Contributed to Rising Loan Defaults." *Brookings Papers on Economic Activity*, 2015.

19-12. McKinsey Global Institute. *Jobs Lost, Jobs Gained: Workforce Transitions in a Time of Automation*. McKinsey & Company, 2017.

19-13. Organisation for Economic Co-operation and Development. *Getting Skills Right: Future-Ready Adult Learning Systems*. OECD Publishing, 2019.

19-15. National Skills Coalition. *United States' Forgotten Middle-Skill Jobs*. National Skills Coalition, 2020, https://nationalskillscoalition.org/resource/publications/.

19-17. Autor, David H. "Work of the Past, Work of the Future." *AEA Papers and Proceedings*, vol. 109, 2019, pp. 1–32.

19-19. Congressional Budget Office. *The Distribution of Household Income, 1989 to 2019*. CBO, 2021, https://www.cbo.gov/publication/58781.

19-20. Organisation for Economic Co-operation and Development. *Adult Learning Participation and Policies: Evidence from OECD Countries*. OECD Publishing, 2021.

19-21. Fuller, Joseph B., and Manjari Raman. *Dismissed by Degrees: How Degree Inflation Is Undermining U.S. Competitiveness and Hurting America's Middle Class*. Harvard Business School, 2017.

20-01. Katz, Lawrence F., and Alan B. Krueger. "The Rise and Nature of Alternative Work Arrangements in the United States, 1995–2015." *ILR Review*, vol. 72, no. 2, 2019, pp. 382–416.

20-02. U.S. Financial Diaries Project. *The Financial Diaries: How American Families Cope in a World of Uncertainty*. Princeton University Press, 2015.

20-03. Bureau of Labor Statistics. *National Compensation Survey: Employee Benefits in the United States, 2023*. U.S. Department of Labor, 2024, https://www.bls.gov/ncs/.

20-04. Congressional Budget Office. *Health Insurance Coverage in the United States: 2023*. CBO, 2024, https://www.cbo.gov/.

20-05. Azar, José, Ioana Marinescu, and Marshall Steinbaum. "Labor Market Concentration." *Journal of Human Resources*, vol. 57, no. S, 2022, pp. S167–S199.

20-06. Bureau of Labor Statistics. *Union Members Summary, 2024*. U.S. Department of Labor, 2025, https://www.bls.gov/news.release/union2.nr0.htm.

20-07. Starr, Evan, J.J. Prescott, and Norman Bishara. "Noncompete Agreements in the U.S. Labor Force." *Journal of Law and Economics*, vol. 64, no. 1, 2021, pp. 53–84.

20-08. OECD. *Employment Outlook 2023*. Organisation for Economic Co-operation and Development, 2023.

20-09. Board of Governors of the Federal Reserve System. *Report on the Economic Well-Being of U.S. Households in 2023*. Federal Reserve, 2024, https://www.federalreserve.gov/.

20-10. Bureau of Labor Statistics. *Labor Force Statistics from the Current Population Survey*. U.S. Department of Labor, 2025, https://www.bls.gov/cps/.

20-11. U.S. Census Bureau. *National Population Projections*. U.S. Department of Commerce, 2023, https://www.census.gov/.

20-12. Congressional Budget Office. *The Demographic Outlook: 2024 to 2054*. CBO, 2024, https://www.cbo.gov/publication/59710.

20-13. Autor, David H., and Mark Duggan. "The Rise in the Disability Rolls and the Decline in Unemployment." *Quarterly Journal of Economics*, vol. 118, no. 1, 2003, pp. 157–205.

20-14. Blau, David, and Janet Currie. "Pre-School, Day Care, and After-School Care: Who's Minding the Kids?" *Handbook of the Economics of Education*, vol. 2, 2006, pp. 1163–1278.

20-15. Krueger, Alan B. "Where Have All the Workers Gone? An Inquiry into the Decline of the U.S. Labor Force Participation Rate." *Brookings Papers on Economic Activity*, 2017.

20-21. Pew Research Center. "Attendance at Religious Services - Religion in America: U.S. Religious Data, Demographics and Statistics." 2023. Pew Research Center. https://www.pewresearch.org/.

20-22. Public Religion Research Institute. "The State of American Churches." 2023. PRRI. https://www.prri.org/.

20-23. Gallup. "U.S. Church Attendance Still Lower Than Pre-Pandemic." 2023. https://www.gallup.com/.

20-24. IslamReligion.com. "Rights of Non-Muslims in Islam (Part 1 of 13)." [n.d.]. https://www.islamreligion.com/articles/394/rights-of-non-muslims-in-islam-part-11/.

20-25. AlIslam.org. "Does Islam Teach Muslims to Hate Non-Believers?" [n.d.]. https://www.alislam.org/articles/does-islam-teach-muslims-to-hate-non-believers/.

20-26. IslamReligion.com. "Rights of Non-Muslims in Islam (Part 1 of 13)." [n.d.]. https://www.islamreligion.com/articles/394/rights-of-non-muslims-in-islam-part-11/.

20-27. Pew Research Center. "Muslim Publics Share Concerns about Extremist Groups." 10 Sep. 2013. https://www.pewresearch.org/global/2013/09/10/muslim-publics-share-concerns-about-extremist-groups/.

20-28. Guttmacher Institute. "About Half of U.S. Abortion Patients Report Using Contraception in the Month They Became Pregnant." Guttmacher Institute, 11 Jan. 2018, www.guttmacher.org/news-release/2018/about-half-us-abortion-patients-report-using-contraception-month-they-became.

20-29. Bradley, Sarah. "When can my baby survive outside the womb?" BabyCenter, 15 Sept. 2022, www.babycenter.com/health/premature-babies/fetal-viability-by-week-what-age-is-the-age-of-viability_40005764.

21-01. International Federation of Robotics. *World Robotics 2024: Industrial Robots (Executive Summary)*. IFR, Sept. 2024, https://ifr.org/img/worldrobotics/Executive_Summary_WR_2024_Industrial_Robots.pdf.

21-02. International Federation of Robotics. "Global Robot Density in Factories Doubled in Seven Years." *IFR Press Releases*, 20 Nov. 2024, https://ifr.org/ifr-press-releases/news/global-robot-density-in-factories-doubled-in-seven-years.

21-04. International Organization for Standardization. *ISO 10218-1:2025, Robotics — Safety Requirements for Industrial Robots — Part 1: Robots*. ISO, 2025, https://www.iso.org/standard/73933.html.

21-05. International Organization for Standardization. *ISO/TS 15066:2016, Robots and Robotic Devices — Collaborative Robots*. ISO, 2016, https://www.iso.org/standard/62996.html.

21-06. NVIDIA. "NVIDIA Announces Project GR00T Foundation Model for Humanoid Robots and Major Isaac Robotics Platform Update." *Press Release*, 18 Mar. 2024, https://investor.nvidia.com/news/press-release-details/2024/NVIDIA-Announces-Project-GR00T-Foundation-Model-for-Humanoid-Robots-and-Major-Isaac-Robotics-Platform-Update/default.aspx.

21-08. Amazon. "Amazon Has More Than 1 Million Robots That Sort, Lift, and Carry Packages." *About Amazon*, 2024, https://www.aboutamazon.com/news/operations/amazon-robotics-robots-fulfillment-center.

21-10. International Data Corporation. *Worldwide Global DataSphere Forecast, 2023–2027: Data Growth and Trends*. Framingham, MA, IDC, 2023, https://www.idc.com/getdoc.jsp?containerId=US50230223.

21-11. Brynjolfsson, Erik, and Andrew McAfee. *The Second Machine Age: Work, Progress, and Prosperity in a Time of Brilliant Technologies*. New York, W. W. Norton & Company, 2014.

21-12. Varian, Hal R. "Beyond Big Data." *Business Economics*, vol. 54, no. 1, Jan. 2019, pp. 27–31, https://doi.org/10.1057/s11369-018-0098-2.

21-13. Zuboff, Shoshana. *The Age of Surveillance Capitalism: The Fight for a Human Future at the New Frontier of Power*. New York, PublicAffairs, 2019.

21-14. Identity Theft Resource Center. *2024 Data Breach Report*. San Diego, CA, Identity Theft Resource Center, 2025, https://www.idtheftcenter.org/publication/2024-data-breach-report/. Accessed 27 Feb. 2026.

21-15. European Union. *Regulation (EU) 2016/679 of the European Parliament and of the Council of 27 April 2016 on the Protection of Natural Persons with Regard to the Processing of Personal Data and on the Free Movement of Such Data (General Data Protection Regulation). Official Journal of the European Union*, L119, 4 May 2016, https://eur-lex.europa.eu/eli/reg/2016/679/oj.

21-16. Manyika, James, et al. *Jobs Lost, Jobs Gained: Workforce Transitions in a Time of Automation*. McKinsey Global Institute, Dec. 2017, https://www.mckinsey.com/featured-insights/future-of-work/jobs-lost-jobs-gained-workforce-transitions-in-a-time-of-automation.

21-17. Acemoglu, Daron, and Pascual Restrepo. "Artificial Intelligence, Automation, and Work." *NBER Working Paper No. 24196*, National Bureau of Economic Research, Jan. 2018, https://doi.org/10.3386/w24196.

21-18. Karabarbounis, Loukas, and Brent Neiman. "The Global Decline of the Labor Share." *Quarterly Journal of Economics*, vol. 129, no. 1, Feb. 2014, pp. 61–103, https://doi.org/10.1093/qje/qjt032.

22. Kelly, Kevin. "The New Socialism." Wikipedia, Wikimedia Foundation, Aug. 2023, en.wikipedia.org/wiki/The_New_Socialism, p. 23.

22-01. Gould, Eric D., Bruce A. Weinberg, and David B. Mustard. "Crime Rates and Local Labor Market Opportunities in the United States: 1979–1997." *Review of Economics and Statistics*, vol. 84, no. 1, Feb. 2002, pp. 45–61, https://doi.org/10.1162/003465302317331919.

22-02. Sampson, Robert J., and W. Byron Groves. “Community Structure and Crime: Testing Social-Disorganization Theory.” *American Journal of Sociology*, vol. 94, no. 4, Jan. 1989, pp. 774–802, https://doi.org/10.1086/229068.

22-03. Federal Bureau of Investigation. *Crime in the United States 2023*. Washington, DC, U.S. Department of Justice, 2024, https://cde.ucr.cjis.gov/LATEST/webapp/#/pages/explorer/crime/crime-trend.

22-04. Centers for Disease Control and Prevention. “Anxiety and Depression: Household Pulse Survey.” CDC, 2024, https://www.cdc.gov/nchs/covid19/pulse/mental-health.htm.

22-05. Ruhm, Christopher J. “Are Recessions Good for Your Health?” *Quarterly Journal of Economics*, vol. 115, no. 2, May 2000, pp. 617–650, https://doi.org/10.1162/003355300554872.

22-06. U.S. Congressional Budget Office. *The Safety Net in the Wake of the Pandemic*. Washington, DC, CBO, 2023, https://www.cbo.gov/publication/58854.

22-07. Cherlin, Andrew J. *Labor's Love Lost: The Rise and Fall of the Working-Class Family in America*. New York, Russell Sage Foundation, 2014.

22-08. Centers for Disease Control and Prevention. *Drug Overdose Deaths in the United States, 2000–2023*. CDC, 2024, https://www.cdc.gov/nchs/pressroom/sosmap/drug_poisoning_mortality/drug_poisoning.htm.

22-09. Case, Anne, and Angus Deaton. *Deaths of Despair and the Future of Capitalism*. Princeton, NJ, Princeton University Press, 2020.

22-10. Federal Reserve Board. *Distribution of Household Wealth in the U.S. since 1989*. Washington, DC, Board of Governors of the Federal Reserve System, 2024, https://www.federalreserve.gov/releases/z1/dataviz/dfa/distribute/chart/.

22-11. Board of Governors of the Federal Reserve System. *Report on the Economic Well-Being of U.S. Households in 2023*. Washington, DC, Federal Reserve, May 2024, https://www.federalreserve.gov/publications/2024-economic-well-being-of-us-households.htm.

22-12. Chetty, Raj, et al. "The Fading American Dream: Trends in Absolute Income Mobility Since 1940." *Science*, vol. 356, no. 6336, Apr. 2017, pp. 398–406, https://doi.org/10.1126/science.aal4617.

22-13. Wilkinson, Richard G., and Kate Pickett. *The Spirit Level: Why Greater Equality Makes Societies Stronger*. New York, Bloomsbury Press, 2009.

22-14. Congressional Budget Office. *The Distribution of Household Income, 1989 to 2019*. Washington, DC, CBO, 2021, https://www.cbo.gov/publication/58781.

22-15. Karabarbounis, Loukas, and Brent Neiman. "The Global Decline of the Labor Share." *Quarterly Journal of Economics*, vol. 129, no. 1, Feb. 2014, pp. 61–103, https://doi.org/10.1093/qje/qjt032.

22-16. Chetty, Raj, Nathaniel Hendren, Patrick Kline, and Emmanuel Saez. "Where Is the Land of Opportunity? The Geography of Intergenerational Mobility in the United States." *Quarterly Journal of Economics*, vol. 129, no. 4, Nov. 2014, pp. 1553–1623, https://doi.org/10.1093/qje/qju022.

22-17. Edelman. *Edelman Trust Barometer 2024*. Chicago, IL, Edelman, 2024, https://www.edelman.com/trust/2024/trust-barometer.

22-18. Pew Research Center. *Public Trust in Government: 1958–2024*. Washington, DC, Pew Research Center, 2024, https://www.pewresearch.org/politics/2024/06/24/public-trust-in-government-1958-2024/.

22-19. Algan, Yann, and Pierre Cahuc. "Trust and Growth." *Annual Review of Economics*, vol. 5, 2013, pp. 521–549, https://doi.org/10.1146/annurev-economics-081412-103333.

22-20. Gilens, Martin, and Benjamin I. Page. "Testing Theories of American Politics: Elites, Interest Groups, and Average Citizens." *Perspectives on Politics*, vol. 12, no. 3, Sept. 2014, pp. 564–581, https://doi.org/10.1017/S1537592714001595.

23. Dahl, Robert A., and Seymour Martin Lipset. Who Governs? August 2023, p. 29.
https://en.wikipedia.org/wiki/Who_Governs%3F.

23-01. U.S. Consumer Product Safety Commission. *About CPSC.* Bethesda, MD, U.S. Consumer Product Safety Commission, 2024, https://www.cpsc.gov/About-CPSC. Accessed 28 Feb. 2026.

23-02. Financial Crisis Inquiry Commission. *The Financial Crisis Inquiry Report: Final Report of the National Commission on the Causes of the Financial and Economic Crisis in the United States.* Washington, DC, U.S. Government Printing Office, 2011, https://www.govinfo.gov/content/pkg/GPO-FCIC/pdf/GPO-FCIC.pdf.

23-03. *Consumer Financial Protection Bureau v. Community Financial Services Association of America, Ltd.*, 601 U.S. ___ (2024). Supreme Court of the United States, https://www.supremecourt.gov/opinions/23pdf/22-448_o7jp.pdf. Accessed 28 Feb. 2026.

23-04. Internal Revenue Service. *SOI Tax Stats — Individual Income Tax Rates and Shares, 2020.* Washington, DC, U.S. Department of the Treasury, 2023, https://www.irs.gov/statistics/soi-tax-stats-individual-income-tax-rates-and-shares. Accessed 28 Feb. 2026.

23-05. Jefferson, Thomas. "To George Washington, 14 Aug. 1787." *Founders Online*, National Archives, https://founders.archives.gov/documents/Jefferson/01-12-02-0284. Accessed 28 Feb. 2026.

23-06. Jefferson, Thomas. "To James Madison, 20 Dec. 1784." *Founders Online*, National Archives, https://founders.archives.gov/documents/Jefferson/01-07-02-0201. Accessed 28 Feb. 2026.

23-07. Jefferson, Thomas. "To James Madison, 6 Sept. 1789." *Founders Online*, National Archives, https://founders.archives.gov/documents/Jefferson/01-15-02-0309. Accessed 28 Feb. 2026.

23-08. Jefferson, Thomas. "First Inaugural Address, 4 Mar. 1801." *Founders Online*, National Archives, https://founders.archives.gov/documents/Jefferson/01-33-02-0112. Accessed 28 Feb. 2026.

23-09. Jefferson, Thomas. "To Samuel Kercheval, 12 July 1816." *Founders Online*, National Archives, https://founders.archives.gov/documents/Jefferson/03-10-02-0198. Accessed 28 Feb. 2026.

23-10. Internal Revenue Service. *IRS Data Book, 2024*. Washington, DC, U.S. Department of the Treasury, 2025, https://www.irs.gov/statistics/soi-tax-stats-irs-data-book. Accessed 28 Feb. 2026.

23-11. Congressional Budget Office. *Monthly Budget Review: Summary for Fiscal Year 2024*. Washington, DC, Congressional Budget Office, Oct. 2024, https://www.cbo.gov/publication/60570. Accessed 28 Feb. 2026.

23-12. Amiti, Mary, Stephen J. Redding, and David E. Weinstein. "The Impact of the 2018 Tariffs on Prices and Welfare." *Journal of Economic Perspectives*, vol. 33, no. 4, Fall 2019, pp. 187–210, https://doi.org/10.1257/jep.33.4.187.

23-13. Congressional Budget Office. *Federal Revenues by Source, 1940 to 2024*. Washington, DC, Congressional Budget Office, 2025, https://www.cbo.gov/data/budget-economic-data. Accessed 28 Feb. 2026.

23-14. U.S. Consumer Product Safety Commission. *About CPSC.* U.S. Consumer Product Safety Commission, 2024, https://www.cpsc.gov/About-CPSC. Accessed 3 Mar. 2026.

23-15. U.S. Consumer Product Safety Commission. *The Consumer Product Safety Act: A History of the CPSC.* U.S. Consumer Product Safety Commission, 2023, https://www.cpsc.gov/s3fs-public/pdfs/blk_media_cpsahistory.pdf. Accessed 3 Mar. 2026.

23-16. Maronick, Thomas J. "Consumer Product Safety and the Role of the Consumer Product Safety Commission." *Journal of Consumer Affairs*, vol. 26, no. 1, 1992, pp. 28–52.

23-17. Financial Crisis Inquiry Commission. *The Financial Crisis Inquiry Report: Final Report of the National Commission on the Causes of the Financial and Economic Crisis in the United States.* U.S. Government Printing Office, 2011.

23-18. Khan, Lina M. "Amazon's Antitrust Paradox." *Yale Law Journal*, vol. 126, no. 3, 2017, pp. 710–805.

23-19. Autor, David, et al. "The Fall of the Labor Share and the Rise of Superstar Firms." *Quarterly Journal of Economics*, vol. 135, no. 2, 2020, pp. 645–709.

59-30. Federal Reserve History. "The Second Bank of the United States." Federal Reserve History, Federal Reserve Bank of San Francisco, www.federalreservehistory.org/essays/second_bank_of_the_united_states.

59-31. United States Inflation Rate, 1946-2021. MacroTrends, www.macrotrends.net/countries/USA/united-states/inflation-rate-cpi. Accessed 2 Mar. 2024.

72-01 Author [Charles Patton] enhanced with added traits.

73. "Federal Election Campaign Act." Answers.com. [September 2023]. http://www.answers.com/topic/federal-election-campaign-act.

74. "Politics of Venezuela." Wikipedia, Wikimedia Foundation, [September 2023]. http://en.wikipedia.org/wiki/Politics_of_Venezuela.

75. "Spain–United States Relations." Wikipedia, Wikimedia Foundation, [September 2023]. http://en.wikipedia.org/wiki/Spain–United_States_relations.

129-02. "U.S. Petroleum Net Imports." U.S. Energy Information Administration. https://www.eia.gov/dnav/pet/hist/LeafHandler.ashx?n=pet&s=mttntus2&f=m. and
"Petroleum Products Net Imports." U.S. Energy Information Administration. https://www.eia.gov/dnav/pet/hist/LeafHandler.ashx?n=pet&s=mttntus2&f=m. and
"FAQ: How much petroleum does the United States import and export?" American Geosciences Institute. https://www.americangeosciences.org/critical-issues/faq/how-much-oil-does-us-export-and-import.

129-03. Republican National Committee. "2016 Republican Party Platform." Republican National Convention, Cleveland, OH, 18-21 July 2016.

129-04. "Social Security Trust Fund depletion date is 2034 without action." Financial Planning. October 2023. https://www.financial-planning.com. and
"Social Security's Financial Outlook: The 2023 Update in Perspective." Center for Retirement Research at Boston College, 2023. https://crr.bc.edu. and
"The Ratio of Workers to Social Security Beneficiaries Is at a Low and Projected to Decline Further." Peter G. Peterson Foundation. October 2023. https://www.pgpf.org.

129-05. Democratic National Committee. "Creating a 21st Century Immigration System." Democrats.org. October 2023 https://democrats.org/where-we-stand/the-issues/immigration-reform/.

129-06 Democratic Platform. "Where we stand on Immigration." Democrats.org. https://democrats.org/where-we-stand/the-issues/immigration-reform/

129-07. "Republicans and Democrats Have Different Top Priorities for U.S. Immigration Policy." Pew Research Center. October 2023. https://www.pewresearch.org/short-reads/2022/09/08/republicans-and-democrats-have-different-top-priorities-for-u-s-immigration-policy/.

129-08. "Republican and Democratic Party Platforms Reflect Parallel Universes on Immigration Policy." Migration Policy Institute. October 2023. https://www.migrationpolicy.org/article/republican-and-democratic-party-platforms-reflect-parallel-universes-immigration-policy.

129-09. "Republicans' Perspectives on Immigration." Politicsphere.com. October 2023. https://www.politicsphere.com/republicans-perspectives-on-immigration/.

139-01: Pew Research Center. "Views on Voting by Mail." Pew Research Center, 13 Oct. 2020, www.pewresearch.org/politics/2020/10/13/views-on-voting-by-mail/.

139-02. Texas v. Johnson, 491 U.S. 397. Supreme Court of the United States. 21 June 1989.

172-02. Jefferson, Thomas. "Reply to Vermont Address." Washington ed., vol. 4, p. 418. Washington, 1801.

173-02. Jefferson, Thomas. "To F. Hopkinson." Washington ed., vol. 2, p. 586; Ford ed., vol. 5, p. 76. Paris, Mar. 1789.

174-02. TITLE: Preface to Tracy's Political Economy, EDITION: Washington ed. Vi, 570, PLACE: [none given], DATE: 1816

175-02. Jefferson, Thomas. "First Annual Message." Washington ed., vol. 8, p. 9; Ford ed., vol. 8, p. 119.

176-02. Jefferson, Thomas. "To Samuel Smith." Washington ed., vol. 7, p. 285; Ford ed., vol. 10, p. 252. Monticello, 1823.

177-02. Jefferson, Thomas. "To J. W. Eppes." Washington ed., vol. 6, p. 195; Ford ed., vol. 9, p. 395. Poplar Forest, Va., Sep. 1813.

178-02. Jefferson, Thomas. "Second Annual Message." Washington ed., vol. 8, p. 21; Ford ed., vol. 8, p. 187. Dec. 1802. EDITION: Ford ed., viii, 187, DATE: Dec. 1802

180-02-b. Jefferson, Thomas. "Autobiography." Washington ed., vol. 1, p. 36; Ford ed., vol. 1, p. 49. 1821.

181-02. Jefferson, Thomas. "To John Adams." Washington ed., vol. 6, p. 224; Ford ed., vol. 9, p. 426. Monticello, 1813.

181-03. "Andrew Jackson." Wikipedia, Wikimedia Foundation, October 2023. http://en.wikipedia.org/wiki/Andrew_Jackson.

181-04. "End the Fed." The Foundation for Rational Economics and Education, Inc. (FREE), Grand Central Publishing, Hachette Book Group, 2009.

181-05. "Independent Treasury System." Wikipedia, Wikimedia Foundation, October 2023. http://en.wikipedia.org/wiki/Independent_Treasury_System.

181-06. "Calculate Carbon Footprint." The Carbon Company. October 2023. http://www.carboncompany.com/calculate-carbon-footprint.

181-07. "Passenger Vehicles in the United States." Wikipedia, Wikimedia Foundation, October 2023. http://en.wikipedia.org/wiki/Passenger_vehicles_in_the_United_States.

181-08. "What is the total number of lawyers in the US?" WikiAnswers. October 2023. http://wiki.answers.com/Q/What_is_the_total_number_of_lawyers_in_the_US.

181-09. "Jefferson's Wall of Separation Letter." U.S. Constitution Online. October 2023. http://www.usConstitution.net/jeffwall.html.

181-10. Google Answers. October 2023.

181-11. "Russian Submarines." CNN. [August 2009]. http://www.cnn.com/2009/US/08/05/russian.submarines/index.html.

184. "Current Numbers." Center for Immigration Studies, [November 2023]. http://www.cis.org/CurrentNumbers.

185. "U.S. Immigration Policy Likely to Boost Population." YaleGlobal Online, [November 2023]. http://yaleglobal.yale.edu/content/us-immigration-policy-likely-boost-population.

317. Limberg, Julian, et al. "50 Years of Tax Cuts for the Rich Have Failed to Trickle Down." The London Economic, 10 Nov. 2024, www.thelondoneconomic.com/news/50-years-of-tax-cuts-for-the-rich-have-failed-to-trickle-down-192664/.

318. Zidar, Owen. "Arguments and Evidence Against Trickle-Down Economics." Profolus, www.profolus.com/topics/arguments-and-evidence-against-trickle-down-economics/.

319. "It's Not Trickling Down: New Data Provides No Evidence That the TCJA Is Working as Its Proponents Claimed It Would." Economic Policy Institute, www.epi.org/publication/its-not-trickling-down-new-data-provides-no-evidence-that-the-tcja-is-working-as-its-proponents-claimed-it-would/.
400. Federal Reserve Bank of St. Louis. "Commercial Real Estate in Focus: Trends and Market Dynamics." Federal Reserve Bank of St. Louis, May 2024, https://www.stlouisfed.org/on-the-economy/2024/may/commercial-real-estate-in-focus. Accessed 20 Feb. 2025.

547. *Citizens United v. Federal Election Commission*, 558 U.S. 310 (2010).

548. Federal Election Commission. *Independent Expenditure Totals by Election Cycle*. Federal Election Commission, 2021, www.fec.gov.

549. OpenSecrets. *Federal Lobbying Spending Totals, 2023*. Center for Responsive Politics, 2024, www.opensecrets.org.

551. U.S. Bureau of Labor Statistics. *Union Members Summary, 2023*. U.S. Department of Labor, 2024, www.bls.gov.

552. Federal Communications Commission. *Media Ownership Rules and Consolidation Data*. Federal Communications Commission, 2023, www.fcc.gov.

www.ingramcontent.com/pod-product-compliance
Lightning Source LLC
LaVergne TN
LVHW090549110826
845146LV00001B/77

9798995852704